Heathe

JOHN KILLEN was born in Belfast in 1954 and was educate[d]
Belfast. Since 1977 he has been a librarian at the Linen Ha[ll]
organised exhibitions on a wide variety of themes, some
displayed in the National Library of Ireland. He has l
historical subjects in Britain and the USA and is a regular contributor to the *Linen Hall Review* and *Irish Booklore*. His publications include *John Bull's Famous Circus, The Irish Christmas Book, The Pure Drop: A Book of Irish Drinking, A History of the Linen Hall Library* and *The Famine Decade: Contemporary Accounts, 1841–1851*.

The

DECADE

of the

UNITED
IRISHMEN

CONTEMPORARY ACCOUNTS

1791–1801

edited by
John Killen

THE
BLACKSTAFF
PRESS

BELFAST

First published in 1997 by
The Blackstaff Press Limited
3 Galway Park, Dundonald, Belfast BT16 0AN, Northern Ireland
Reprinted 1998

© This collection and Introduction, John Killen, 1997
Typeset by Techniset Typesetters, Newton-le-Willows, Merseyside

Printed in England by Biddles Limited

A CIP catalogue record for this book
is available from the British Library

ISBN 0-85640-611-2

ACKNOWLEDGEMENTS

The editor wishes to thank the governors of the Linen Hall Library for their encouragement and support at all times; also, Dr Christopher Woods and Irish Academic Press for allowing the use of two extracts from *The Journals of Thomas Russell*; and the Deputy Keeper of the Records, Public Record Office of Northern Ireland, for allowing the use of two letters from the *Drennan Letters*.

CONTENTS

INTRODUCTION   1

1 7 9 1

Without Enthusiasm Nothing Great Was Done
   DR WILLIAM DRENNAN   13
Declaration of the Rights of Man and of Citizens   THOMAS PAINE   14
To the People   *An Argument on Behalf of the Catholics of Ireland*   18
Declaration and Resolutions of the Society of United Irishmen
   of Belfast   THEOBALD WOLFE TONE   20
United Irishmen of Dublin   JAMES NAPPER TANDY, *Belfast
   News-Letter*   22

1 7 9 2 – 1 7 9 4

No Fear but that of Forfeiture   WILLIAM TODD JONES   27
United Irishmen   *Belfast News-Letter*   28
Dethronement of Louis XVI   *Northern Star*   29
Address from the Society of United Irishmen, in Dublin, to the
   Delegates for Promoting a Reform in Scotland
   Belfast News-Letter   30
The Catholic Petition
   THE PETITION OF THE CATHOLICS OF IRELAND   31
National Convention   *Northern Star*   32
Execution of Louis XVI   *Northern Star*   33
Lord Bayham to the Honourable Robert Stewart
   Memoirs and Correspondence of Viscount Castlereagh   35
War   *Hansard's Parliamentary Debates*   36
Catholic Relief   AN ACT FOR THE RELIEF OF HIS MAJESTY'S POPISH
   OR ROMAN CATHOLIC SUBJECTS OF IRELAND   37
It Will End in Republicanism   *Journals of Thomas Russell*   40
The State of the Country   *Northern Star*   43
The Society of United Irishmen to the Hon. Simon Butler and
   Oliver Bond, Esqr.   *Belfast News-Letter*   44
Vast Majority Would Join the French   *Journals of Thomas Russell*   44
The Hopes of France Utterly Disappointed
   Journals of the House of Commons, Ireland   47
Mr Hamilton Rowan   *Northern Star*   48
Plan for More Completely Providing for the Security of the Country
   Hansard's Parliamentary Debates   49

The King Against M'Cabe and Others, Publishers and Proprietors
    of a Newspaper Called, *Northern Star*   *Belfast News-Letter*   50
Arrangements in Ireland   *Belfast News-Letter*   51

1795–1797

Protestant Dissenters' Address   *Northern Star*   55
Roman Catholic Emancipation   *Belfast News-Letter*   55
The Exiled Irishman's Lamentation   *Paddy's Resource*   56
Earl Fitzwilliam's Departure   *Northern Star*   58
Union   *Northern Star*   59
The Reverend William Jackson   *Walker's Hibernian Magazine*   60
Theobald Wolfe Tone   *Northern Star*   60
Unite and Be Free   *Paddy's Resource*   61
Athy Assizes   *Belfast News-Letter*   62
Extract of a Letter from a Gentleman in the Neighbourhood
    of Armagh   *Belfast News-Letter*   63
Prelude to the Formation of the Orange Order   *Northern Star*   64
Tone Arrives in France   *Journals of Theobald Wolfe Tone*   64
Dublin   *Belfast News-Letter*   69
To the People of Ireland   A LETTER ON THE STATE OF PARTIES
    AND ON THE SUBJECT OF REFORM, ADDRESSED TO THE PEOPLE   69
The Union of Irishmen   *Northern Star*   70
Orangemen Capitally Convicted   *The Sun*   71
To the United Irishmen   *Northern Star*   71
Tone's Birthday   *Journals of Theobald Wolfe Tone*   73
Ordnance for Belfast   *The Sun*   74
Preparations   *Journals of Theobald Wolfe Tone*   74
The Felony Act   AN ACT MORE EFFECTUALLY TO SUPPRESS
    INSURRECTIONS, AND PREVENT THE DISTURBANCE OF THE
    PUBLICK PEACE   76
Army of the Rhine and the Moselle   *Northern Star*   78
Equality, Fraternity and Oppression
    A Frenchman's Walk Through Ireland, 1796–1797   80
Arrest of Neilson and Russell   MRS MARTHA McTIER   81
Arrest of William Orr   *Belfast News-Letter*   82
The Threatened Invasion   *Hansard's Parliamentary Debates*   82
McCracken and Keenan Committed on a Charge of High Treason
    The Times   84
Lord Malmesbury to Lord Grenville   *Diaries and Correspondence of*
    James Harris, 1st Earl of Malmesbury   85
The Attempted Invasion of Ireland   *Journals of Theobald Wolfe Tone*   85
Military Preparations   *The Times*   91
Northern Star   *Northern Star*   91

Unwelcome News   *Journals of Theobald Wolfe Tone*   92
A Most Horrid Murder   *The Sun*   93
United Irishmen Imprisoned in Kilmainham   *The Times*   93
Further Report from the Committee of Secrecy
   Journals of the House of Commons, Ireland   94
Letter from Lord Clifden to Lord Colchester
   Diary of Lord Colchester   97
Cornwallis is Sent to Ireland   *Belfast News-Letter*   98
Execution of Four Privates of the Monaghan Militia   *The Times*   98
The Resolutions of the Orange Societies of Ulster
   Belfast News-Letter   99
Capture of Forge for Making Pikes   *The Sun*   100
A Horrid Conspiracy   *The Times*   101
Seditious Practices   *The Times*   102
Arrest of United Irishmen   *Belfast News-Letter*   102
State Prisoners   *The Times*   103
Trial of William Orr, for Imposing Unlawful Oaths   *The Sun*   103
The Dying Declaration of William Orr   *The Press*   104
Vive le Republic   *Journals of Theobald Wolfe Tone*   106

1798

Wake of William Orr   *The Press*   111
The Complexion of the Times   *The Times*   113
News from Ireland   *Journals of Theobald Wolfe Tone*   114
Conduct Best Calculated for Obtaining Victory
   LORD EDWARD FITZGERALD   114
Debate in the Lords on the State of Ireland
   Hansard's Parliamentary Debates   116
So Easy a Situation   MARQUIS CORNWALLIS   119
Limerick Proclaimed   *Belfast News-Letter*   119
Arrest of a Committee of United Irishmen   *The Times*   120
Arrest of Lord Edward Fitzgerald   *The Times*   121
Curfew   *Belfast News-Letter*   121
Arrest of the Sheares   *The Times*   122
Actual Hostilities   MARQUIS CORNWALLIS   123
Martial Law Proclaimed   *Belfast News-Letter*   124
Northern Mail Coach Stopped   *The Times*   125
Safety of the Empire   LORD CASTLEREAGH   126
State of the Country   *Belfast News-Letter*   127
Rebellion in Ireland   *The Times*   127
The North   *Belfast News-Letter*   128
Most Acceptable Military Intelligence   LORD CASTLEREAGH   129
Informer   *The Apostacy of Newell*   130

News from the North   *Belfast News-Letter* 133
Rebellion in the County Antrim   *Belfast News-Letter* 135
News of the Last Importance   *Journals of Theobald Wolfe Tone* 136
Just Objects of Punishment   LORD CASTLEREAGH 138
Severe and Many Examples   LIEUTENANT-GENERAL LAKE 139
The Guilt of Participating in the Wexford Rebellion
   The Times 139
Arrival of Cornwallis   *The Times* 141
The Most Assuring Accounts   *The Times* 142
To Suppress the Folly   MARQUIS CORNWALLIS 143
The Violence of our Friends   MARQUIS CORNWALLIS 143
A State of *Present* Inactivity   MARQUIS CORNWALLIS 144
Court Martial   *Belfast News-Letter* 147
Execution of the Mess. Sheares   *Belfast News-Letter* 147
No Law but Martial Law   MARQUIS CORNWALLIS 148
Downpatrick Assizes   *Belfast News-Letter* 149
To Subdue them or Invite them to Surrender
   MARQUIS CORNWALLIS 150
The Trade of Highwaymen   *The Times* 151
General Court Martial at Carrickfergus   *Belfast News-Letter* 152
To Check the Progress of the Enemy   MARQUIS CORNWALLIS 152
Impossible to Manage the Militia   LIEUTENANT-GENERAL LAKE 153
So Shameful a Rout   EDWARD COOKE, ESQ. 153
Quiet in the North   GENERAL NUGENT 154
Mayo Manifesto   *The Times* 155
Surrender of the French   *Belfast News-Letter* 156
With Regard to Future Plans   MARQUIS CORNWALLIS 157
Bands of Lawless Desperados   *The Times* 158
Union Alone   THE EARL OF CLARE 159
General Humbert to the Executive Directory   *Belfast News-Letter* 160
Four Frigates and a Brig   MARQUIS CORNWALLIS 162
The Arrival of *La Hoche* in Lough Swilly   *Belfast News-Letter* 163
The Heads of the Treaty of Union   THE DUKE OF PORTLAND 163
Theobald Wolfe Tone   *Belfast News-Letter* 165
Nothing but Martial Authority   LORD CASTLEREAGH 166
The Test of their Disposition   THE DUKE OF PORTLAND 167

1799–1801

Union and Anti-Union   *The Times* 171
The Consolidation of the Strength of Both Islands
   RIGHT HONOURABLE THOMAS CONOLLY 171
Rebellion . . . not Dead but Sleepeth   *The Times* 171

The Ascendancy of the Protestant Religion
    THE BISHOP OF LIMERICK   172
The Escape of Dwyer   *The Times*   172
An Unfavourable Turn   MARQUIS CORNWALLIS   173
Fraught with Curses   AN ADDRESS TO THE PEOPLE OF IRELAND
    AGAINST A UNION   174
No Reason to Despair   MARQUIS CORNWALLIS   175
The Most Corrupt People under Heaven   MARQUIS CORNWALLIS   175
Lord Clare's Immediate Promotion   MARQUIS CORNWALLIS   176
In Favour of Union   LIEUTENANT-COLONEL LITTLEHALES   177
The Yoke of a British Parliament   HENRY GRATTAN'S SPEECH TO
    THE HOUSE OF COMMONS   178
More Harm than Good   MARQUIS CORNWALLIS   181
The Union is Carried   MARQUIS CORNWALLIS   181
The Act of Union   AN ACT FOR THE UNION OF GREAT BRITAIN
    AND IRELAND   182

1801–1803

Parliament Meets   FIRST SESSION OF THE FIRST PARLIAMENT OF
    THE UNITED KINGDOM OF GREAT BRITAIN AND IRELAND   187
No Catholic Emancipation   KING GEORGE III   189
To Tranquillize the Minds of the Catholics
    MARQUIS CORNWALLIS   190
Daily Expectation of Rebellion and Invasion
    Diary of Charles Abbot, Lord Colchester   191
A Chance Encounter   *Diary of Earl Mount Cashel*   192
Failure of Peace Negotiations   *Hansard's Parliamentary Debates*   193
Inflammable Materials   LIEUTENANT-COLONEL LITTLEHALES   193
'Love the Brotherhood, Fear God and Honour the King'
    AN ADDRESS OF THE MASTERS OF THE SEVERAL ORANGE
    SOCIETIES IN THE COUNTY OF ANTRIM, 6 JUNE 1803, ON A
    RENEWAL OF THE WAR WITH FRANCE   194
General Statement of the Matters Relating to the Insurrection of
    23 July 1803   *Diary of Lord Castlereagh*   195
The Trial of Emmet   REPORT OF THE TRIAL OF ROBERT EMMET
    UPON AN INDICTMENT FOR HIGH TREASON   200
Emmet's Speech from the Dock   REPORT OF THE TRIAL OF
    ROBERT EMMET UPON AN INDICTMENT FOR HIGH TREASON   204
Report of the Trial of Thomas Russell, a Rebel General During
    the Late Insurrection   *Walker's Hibernian Magazine*   206
Few, Few Have I Known Like Him   MRS MARTHA McTIER   208

INDEX   211

INTRODUCTION

Writing to his brother-in-law on 21 May 1791, Dr William Drennan outlined a plan for founding a secret society dedicated to political reform in Ireland. It should be 'a benevolent conspiracy – a plot for the people . . . the Brotherhood its name – the Rights of Men and the Greatest Happiness of the Greatest Number its end – its general end Real Independence to Ireland, and Republicanism its particular purpose'. In that letter was the genesis of the United Irishmen – the name coined by a young Dublin barrister, Theobald Wolfe Tone. Tone had already involved himself in politics by accepting a commission from the Catholic Committee to write a pamphlet outlining the disabilities under which Catholics laboured because of the system of Penal Laws currently in force. His *Argument on Behalf of the Catholics of Ireland*, published in August 1791, brought Tone to the attention of other radicals, especially the northern Presbyterian radicals of Belfast.

The Society of the United Irishmen was founded on 14 October 1791, in Peggy Barclay's Tavern, Crown Entry, Belfast. Among the founding members were the leading men of Belfast society: William Sinclair, Samuel McTier, Samuel Neilson, Robert and William Simms, Gilbert McIlveen and William Tennent. Tone and his military friend Thomas Russell were sworn in as members and attended the first meeting of the Society of United Irishmen on 18 October 1791. At that meeting a declaration, and set of resolutions, prepared by Tone, were adopted as the *raison d'être* of the society. Tone wrote:

> We think it our duty, as Irishmen, to come forward, and state what we feel to be our heavy grievance, and what we know to be its effectual remedy. WE HAVE NO NATIONAL GOVERNMENT; and we are ruled by Englishmen, and the servants of Englishmen, whose object is the interest of another country, whose instrument is corruption, and whose strength is the weakness of Ireland . . .
>
> [We] require a cordial union among ALL THE PEOPLE OF IRELAND [and] a complete and radical reform of the representation of the people in Parliament . . . [We acknowledge] that no reform is practicable, efficacious, or just, which shall not include Irishmen of every *religious* persuasion.

This *Declaration and Resolutions of the United Irishmen of Belfast* urged the formation of similar societies in other towns in Ireland, the abolition of religious and political bigotry, and an equality of rights and opportunities throughout society. In this, the original founders of the United Irishmen were influenced by the works of the European Englightenment, by the progress of the French Revolution, accounts of which were published daily in the *Belfast News-Letter*, and by Thomas Paine's pamphlet, *The Rights of Man*, published in 1791 as a response to Edmund Burke's *Reflections on the Revolution in France*. This pamphlet was instantly reprinted in Dublin and Belfast and became essential reading matter for the growing number of societies of United Irishmen. In his pamphlet, Paine cited the *Declaration of the Rights of Man and of Citizens*, which had been published by the National Assembly of France. Three fundamental rights underpinned the political philosophy of the United Irishmen:

1 Men are born and always continue free, and equal in respect of their rights.
2 The end of all political associations is the preservation of the natural and imprescriptible rights of man; and these rights are − liberty, property, security and resistance to oppression.
3 The nation is essentially the source of all sovereignty.

These three propositions were fundamentally revolutionary in the Europe of their day, as the unfolding violence and apparent anarchy of the French Revolution confirmed. In England William Pitt's government was keeping a close and increasingly wary eye on developments in France, and feared an inevitable contest in arms against a nation dedicated to exporting revolution throughout Europe. By expounding the principles of revolution − and, ultimately, of armed revolution − the Society of United Irishmen was marked out as a dangerous and subversive association of political malcontents. Its subsequent development and actions were to be routinely monitored and closely checked by the administration in Ireland, and at Westminster.

In the first flush of enthusiasm, the United Irishmen began a propaganda campaign to spread and reinforce their aims. Pamphlets were published and newspapers founded to inform and to politicise the people. Always, and consistently, the twin demands of parliamentary reform and removal of the disabilities of the Catholics were put forward. But there were vested interests which strongly resisted both demands. Rumour abounded that Catholic Emancipation would be a prelude to a general undoing of the land system, with forced forfeiture of land for redistribution to native (and, consequently, Catholic) owners. This fear was always present in the minds of the Protestant Ascendancy, who

understood intimately the Catholic race memory of confiscation,
plantation and penal law. This agrarian undercurrent (an aspiration of
the Catholic secret society, the Defenders) was little understood by the
mainly urban leaders of the United Irishmen, but would emerge in the
motivation of the Wexford insurgents in 1798. Initially, however, the
idea was dismissed as 'unfounded and delusive'. William Todd Jones,
MP for Lisburn and a prolific pamphleteer, challenged anyone with such
information to 'come forward ... and boldly combat and confute' the
stated aspirations of the United Irishmen.

Of more immediate importance was the progress of the revolution in
France. The *Northern Star*, launched in Belfast in January 1792 by a committee of United Irishmen, rejoiced at the rapidity with which the cause
of liberty was making its way through Europe. The dethronement and
subsequent execution of Louis XVI did not dismay them: both events
were reported extensively in the newspaper. By the time that war was
eventually declared between England and France, in February 1793,
leading United Irishmen (and especially Thomas Russell) believed that
there must be a long, bloody and general war that would result in republicanism throughout Europe. Such beliefs were also held by politicians at
Westminster and at Dublin Castle, and motivated them in their response
to the twin demands for parliamentary reform and Catholic Emancipation. The 1793 Act for the Relief of His Majesty's Popish or Roman
Catholic Subjects of Ireland fell far short of the relief that the Catholic
Committee had expected, and resulted in sporadic unrest throughout
the island. The Ascendancy contrived, as a consequence, to block such
reforms as the act allowed. In the new atmosphere of a European war,
government in England and Ireland was determined to suppress dissi-
dents. Simon Butler and Oliver Bond challenged the authority of a
secret committee of the House of Lords, set up to investigate the state
of Ireland, and were promptly jailed for six months and each fined
£500. The proprietors of the *Northern Star* were prosecuted for printing
a 'scandalous and seditious libel' – Tone's *Declaration and Resolutions of the
Society of United Irishmen of Belfast* – and found guilty. Archibald Hamilton Rowan, a major landowner, barrister and United Irishman, was
arrested, tried for treason, and found guilty. He was sentenced to two
years' imprisonment and fined £500. Rowan's conviction and sentence
indicated the Government's determination to pursue the United Irishmen as ruthlessly as possible, despite the fact that he later escaped from
prison and fled to America.

Drennan was also tried in 1794 for publishing a seditious libel, but acquitted. This ordeal prompted him to renounce revolutionary politics, and he resigned from the United Irishmen. The clampdown on the activities and personnel of the United Irishmen continued throughout 1794 and 1795 and a central tenet of their reform policy was ruthlessly and publicly rejected with the recall of Lord Fitzwilliam on 23 February 1795 in ignominy some three months into his tenure as lord lieutenant because of his espousal of Catholic Emancipation. This, more than any other single event, proved to be the catalyst which transformed the United Irishmen from a group of political reformers into a revolutionary movement dedicated to the separation of Ireland from English rule and influence.

When the French agent the Reverend William Jackson was tried for high treason in 1795, the Society of United Irishmen, and Tone in particular, were implicated. Tone had written a document giving his views on the state of Ireland and how the Irish might react in the event of a French invasion. This document came into the hands of government and when Jackson was found guilty, Tone was marked as a dangerous revolutionary. He thought it expedient to remove himself from Ireland, and to this end he quickly disposed of his property in Kildare and set out for Belfast en route to America. In the northern capital he was fêted by his friends, and reunited with his most intimate friend, Thomas Russell.

On a fine day in May, just prior to the Tones' departure, Tone, Russell, Samuel Neilson, the Simmses, Henry Joy McCracken and a select group of revolutionary friends climbed to McArt's fort on the Cave Hill, overlooking the town of Belfast, and there they pledged themselves 'never to desist in [their] efforts until [they] had subverted the authority of England over [their] country, and asserted [their] independence'. On 12 June 1795 Tone and his family sailed for America. Within a year he was in France, treating with the Directory for a French invasion force to be sent to Ireland.

The situation in Ireland, however, was deteriorating rapidly. The Defenders were actively organising in anticipation of a French invasion. They were engaged in armed clashes with the Protestant secret society, the Peep o' Day Boys; in the wake of just such a bloody encounter in the county of Armagh, the Orange Order was founded. The stated aims of the Orange Order were to preserve the peace of the country, to support the king and constitution, and to maintain the Protestant Ascendancy. Implacable hatred between the Defenders and the Orange Order would soon extend to the United Irishmen, and become a major factor in the polarisation of Irish society.

In February 1796 Tone arrived in France, and made immediately for
Paris where he was granted an audience with Carnot, the 'organiser of victory'. Tone was asked to prepare a report on the state of Ireland and he explained that the Catholics and Dissenters of Ireland were unanimous in favour of the French, and were eager to throw off the yoke of England. He stated that he had been sent as a representative of these two sects to ask for French aid. For the next six months Tone pleaded his case and was alternately elated and depressed by conflicting promises of naval and military support for an uprising in Ireland.

In Ireland, in 1796 and 1797, unrest and sectarian hatred fuelled atrocities. Information was sought and given against Defenders, and Orangemen were not behind hand in exacting vengeance on their Catholic neighbours. Military supplies were dispatched northwards to help contain the situation, and parliament rushed through an act 'more effectively to suppress insurrections'. The progress of the war on the Continent was followed through the pages of the *Northern Star*, and each French victory gave comfort to, and strengthened the resolve of, a revolutionary core of United Irishmen. An ongoing campaign of enticing soldiers to take the oath of the United Irishmen resulted in public floggings and ultimately in executions.

In this atmosphere, government decided to strike against the leaders of the United Irishmen. In September 1796 the Belfast leaders were arrested and taken under armed guard to Dublin. Neilson and Russell surrendered themselves to Lord Castlereagh in the house of the Belfast Society for Promoting Knowledge, and were likewise taken to Dublin. In October, Henry Joy McCracken and James Keenan were taken. At the same time England was preparing to repel an invasion; but the exact destination of a French invasion force was unclear until November 1796 when Lord Malmesbury received information that eleven sail of the line were ready at the French port of Brest, with some fifteen to twenty thousand men on board. Their destination was undoubtedly Ireland.

The French invasion fleet set sail on 15 December, and immediately ran into trouble. By the time Tone's ship, the *Indomptable*, reached Bantry Bay, the fleet was terribly scattered. The weather was so bad that no effective landing was possible, and on 29 December 1796, when the admiral gave the signal to steer for France, the proposed invasion of Ireland was over.

The sight of a French fleet off the coast of Cork created mixed reactions in the hearts and minds of the various factions in Ireland. Volunteer corps were formed, and requests were sent to government to allow for the arming of Orangemen in defence of the country. Government proceeded with a strenuous clampdown on the activities of the United Irishmen. In February 1797 the offices of the *Northern Star* were ransacked and the type and printing press destroyed. Further arrests of United Irishmen took place and in May the Reverend Sinclair Kelburn, Dissenting minister, and Dr Crawford of Lisburn were imprisoned in Kilmainham. A secret committee of the House of Lords identified Tone as the instigator of the Society of United Irishmen, whose extirpation now became a matter of necessity. In September 1797, William Orr, a prosperous County Antrim farmer, was tried under the Insurrection Act for administering the oath of the United Irishmen to soldiers. He was found guilty and hanged at Carrickfergus, despite pleas for clemency from many quarters.

In March 1798 Lord Edward Fitzgerald, the leader and organiser of the proposed rebellion, had his house searched, and among the papers found was a plan of military operations to be undertaken by the United Irishmen in Dublin. This document outlined the tactics to be used by pikemen and riflemen against the militia when the planned rebellion began. In turn, this attack in Dublin would be the signal for a general outbreak of hostilities throughout the country. By discovering this paper, and by the use of informers such as Edward John Newell and Thomas Reynolds, government was appraised of the military plans of the United Irishmen. On 12 March 1798 the Leinster provincial executive of the United Irishmen was arrested at Oliver Bond's house in Dublin, betrayed by Reynolds. In May another committee of United Irishmen was taken at the house of one Magrath, a publican; and on 24 May 1798, Lord Edward Fitzgerald was arrested. Two days later the brothers John and Henry Sheares were also arrested in Dublin. So serious was the situation that martial law was proclaimed, and actual hostilities broke out on 23 May 1798.

Because government knew so much about the plans of the United Irishmen's proposed attack, effective military preparations had already been taken. When fighting began, Lord Castlereagh acknowledged that the rebellion was not uniform over the entire country, and opined that should it remain within its present confines, it would soon be disposed of. He was confident of the outcome and looked to a successful military resolution to the conflict. He also saw that a successful military campaign would extinguish the threat of rebellion in Ireland and would place 'the kingdom, and of course the empire, in a state of security much beyond that in which it has stood for years past'.

And so it proved. The rebellion had three distinct theatres of war: in
the south, in the west, and in the north. Counties Wicklow, Wexford, Kildare, Carlow, Meath and King's County (Offaly) saw fighting, as did Down and Antrim. Later, with the small French invasion force in Connaught, Mayo also saw conflict. By then, however, the military superiority of a reinforced army had defeated and subdued the main forces of the United Irishmen. Hostilities degenerated into a guerrilla warfare, especially in Wicklow with Joseph Holt and Michael Dwyer. The leaders of the insurrection suffered capitally for their rebellion. In the north, McCracken and Henry Munro were hanged. In the south, Lord Edward Fitzgerald died of wounds received during his arrest. The Sheares brothers, Beauchamp Bagenal Harvey, and John Hay were hanged. Others were transported or allowed to go into exile. Tone was captured when he arrived in Lough Swilly aboard a French frigate. He committed suicide in prison.

In the immediate aftermath of the rebellion, the newly appointed lord lieutenant, Lord Cornwallis, set about organising a political union between Great Britain and Ireland. Such a union had been suggested many times throughout the eighteenth century and, within our period, as early as 1791, the same year as Tone's *Argument on Behalf of the Catholics of Ireland*, as a means of strengthening and protecting the Empire, but such a measure was fraught with difficulties. Opinion in favour of union in early 1799 was not strong enough to attempt to pass such a measure. A concerted campaign of persuasion, intimidation and bribery was necessary to obtain a majority in the Irish parliament in favour of union. Lord Castlereagh and Lord Cornwallis spent twelve exacting months in that campaign, at times despairing of the result being achieved, and they deplored the mendacity of the people with whom they had to contend. Deals had to be done with bishops, politicians, lords (both Catholic and Protestant) and others to facilitate the policy of union – and all this while outbreaks of unrest and fighting were taking place throughout disaffected areas. Cornwallis in particular disliked the business and only kept on with the campaign because of his belief that without a union 'the British Empire must be dissolved'. He lamented his lot: 'negotiating and jobbing with the most corrupt people under heaven'. But eventually, on 18 February 1800, the Union was carried in the Irish House of Commons. The act was given the royal assent on the first day of August 1800, but not before Henry Grattan had wounded the Chancellor of the Irish Exchequer, Isaac Corry, in a duel in the Phoenix Park for an insult made during the course of the debate.

The first meeting of the newly created imperial parliament took place on 22 January 1801, and George III in his speech to the House of Lords expressed 'his satisfaction, at such a crucial time in the European war, to avail himself of the advice and assistance of the parliament of his United Kingdom of Great Britain and Ireland'.

Cornwallis had hinted to Catholic peers that in return for their vote for the Union, government would expedite Catholic Emancipation in the new parliament. His hopes for such a measure were dashed almost simultaneously with the passing of the Act of Union when it became clear that George III would not countenance such a concession under any circumstances. Cornwallis had to make the best of things and set out to 'tranquillize the minds of the Catholics'.

Meanwhile the European war was moving towards a treaty of peace, and in October 1801 hostilities between France and England were suspended. This opened up the prospect of limited European travel, and in March 1802, Stephen, 2nd Earl Mount Cashel, had a chance encounter in Paris with a young man who had been 'amongst the politically distinguished in Dublin College'. They met at the house of an English gentleman, because of the young Dubliner's 'extreme prejudice against French society'. The young man was Robert Emmet, and he was in France seeking aid for a second invasion and rebellion in Ireland. There he met with Thomas Russell, recently released from Fort George in Scotland.

Within fourteen months of this encounter the fragile peace had been broken and France and England were again at war. Emmet returned to Dublin and Russell followed. There they laid plans for an insurrection in Dublin and in the north on 23 July 1803. In Dublin, Emmet's band of followers melted away in the face of resistance from troops from Cork Street Barracks. Arthur Wolfe, 1st Viscount Kilwarden, and Lord Chief Justice of Ireland, with his nephew Colonel Browne, were taken from their carriage as they made their way into Dublin on the evening of 23 July 1803 and were killed by a small band of insurgents. Emmet was later arrested and tried for high treason; he was found guilty and was executed on 20 September 1803. One month later Russell stood trial for the same offence in the courthouse in Downpatrick. His dignity and composure were remarked on by the journalist who recorded the proceedings and justify Martha McTier's trenchant remark, 'Few, few have I known like him'.

With the deaths of Emmet and Russell, the Society of United Irishmen ceased to exist. Their liberal and egalitarian aims of an abolition of bigotry in religion and politics, and an equal distribution of the rights of man through all sects and denominations of Irishmen, came to nought. In the decade which began with the foundation of the Society of United Irishmen and ended with the Act of Union, Irish society was permanently politicised and polarised, distrust and hatred proving more enduring than the idea of a union of Irishmen.

JOHN KILLEN

JUNE 1997

1791

WITHOUT ENTHUSIASM
NOTHING GREAT WAS DONE

Dublin, 21 May 1791

I should much desire that a Society were instituted in this city having much of the secrecy and somewhat of the ceremonial of Freemasonry, so much secrecy as might communicate curiosity, uncertainty, expectation to the minds of surrounding men, so much impressive and affecting ceremony in its internal economy as without impeding real business might strike the soul through the senses. A benevolent conspiracy—a plot for the people—no *Whig* Club—no party title—the Brotherhood its name—the Rights of Men and the Greatest Happiness of the Greatest Number its end—its general end Real Independence to Ireland, and Republicanism its particular purpose—its business every means to accomplish these ends as speedily as the prejudices and bigotry of the land we live in would permit, as speedily as to give us some enjoyment and not to protract anything too long in this short span of life. The means are manifold, publication always coming from one of the Brotherhood,

DR WILLIAM DRENNAN

and no other designation. Declaration, a solemn and religious compact with each other to be signed by every member, and its chief and leading principles to be conveyed into a symbol worn by every of them round their body next the heart. Communication with leading men in France, in England and in America, so as to cement the scattered and shifting sand of republicanism into a body (as well as those malignant conspiracies which courts and classes of men have formed) and when thus cemented to sink it like a caisson in the dark and troubled waters, a stable unseen power. Why should secrecy be necessary? For many reasons. It gives greater energy within, greater influence abroad. It conceals members whose professions, etc., would make concealment expedient until the trial comes, etc., etc. I therefore think and insist on your not even mentioning it, nor do not imagine I shall neglect my profession or injure my character by keeping bad company. You are not, I believe, a republican, but not many years will elapse till this persuasion will prevail, for nothing else but the public happiness as an end, and the public will as the power and means of obtaining it, is good in politics and all else is job. Such schemes are not to be laughed at as romantic, for without enthusiasm nothing great was done, or will be done.

LETTER FROM DR WILLIAM DRENNAN TO SAMUEL M'TIER

21 MAY 1791

DECLARATION OF THE RIGHTS OF MAN AND OF CITIZENS

THOMAS PAINE

There never did, there never will, and there never can exist a parliament, or any description of men, or any generation of men, in any country, possessed of the right or the power of binding and controlling posterity to the "*end of time*," or of commanding for ever how the world shall be governed, or who shall govern it: and therefore all such clauses, acts or declarations, by which the makers of them attempt to do what they have neither the right nor the power to do, nor the power to execute, are in themselves null and void.—Every age and generation must be as free to act for itself, *in all cases*, as the ages and generations which preceded it . . .

Every generation is and must be competent to all the purposes which its occasions require. It is the living, and not the dead, that are to be accommodated . . .

I am not contending for, nor against, any form of government, nor for, nor against, any party here or elsewhere. That which a whole nation chooses to do, it has a right to do . . .

The laws of every country must be analogous to some common principle . . . It requires but a very small glance of thought to perceive, that although laws made in one generation often continue in force through succeeding generations, yet that they continue to derive their force from the consent of the living. A law not repealed continues in force, not because it *cannot* be repealed, but because it *is not* repealed; and the non-repealing passes for consent . . .

The circumstances of the world are continually changing, and the

opinions of men change also; and as government is for the living, and
not for the dead, it is the living only that has any right in it. That which
may be thought right and found convenient in one age, may be thought
wrong and found inconvenient in another.—In such cases, who is to
decide; the living, or the dead? . . .

While I am writing this, there is accidentally before me some
proposals for a declaration of rights by the Marquis de la Fayette . . . to
the National Assembly on the 11th of July, 1789, three days before the
taking of the Bastile; . . . M. de la Fayette applies to the living world, and
emphatically says, "Call to mind the sentiments which Nature has
engraved in the heart of every citizen, and which take a new force when
they are solemnly recognized by all:—For a nation to love liberty, it is
sufficient that she knows it; and to be free, it is
sufficient that she wills it."

It was not against Louis the XVIth, but
against the despotic principles of the government, that the nation revolted. These principles have not their origin in him; but in the
original establishment, many centuries back;
and they were become too deeply rooted to
be removed, and the augean stable of parasites
and plunderers too abominably filthy to be
cleansed, by anything short of a complete
and universal revolution. When it becomes
necessary to do a thing, the whole heart and
soul should go into the measure, or not
attempt it. That crisis was then arrived, and
there remained no choice but to act with
determined vigour, or not to act at all. The
King was known to be the friend of the
nation, and this circumstance was favourable
to the enterprise. Perhaps no man bred up in
the stile of an absolute King, ever possessed a
heart so little disposed to the exercise of that

THOMAS PAINE

species of power as the present King of France. But the principles of the
government itself still remained the same. The Monarch and the Monarchy were distinct and separate things; and it was against the established
despotism of the latter, and not against the person or principles of the
former, that the revolt commenced, and the revolution has been carried
. . . The natural moderation of Louis the XVIth contributed nothing to

alter the hereditary despotism of the monarchy. All the tyranny of former reigns, acted under that hereditary despotism, were still liable to be revived in the hands of a successor. It was not the respite of a reign that would satisfy France, enlightened as she was then become. A casual discontinuance of the *practice* of despotism, is not a discontinuance of its *principles*; the former depends on the virtue of the individual who is in immediate possession of the power; the latter, on the virtue and fortitude of the nation ... Lay then the axe to the root, and teach governments humanity ...

The National Assembly, instead of vindictive proclamations, as has been the case with other governments, published a Declaration of the Rights of Man, as the basis on which the new constitution was to be built, and which is here subjoined.

DECLARATION OF THE RIGHTS OF MAN AND OF CITIZENS

By the NATIONAL ASSEMBLY of FRANCE

The Representatives of the people of FRANCE, formed into a National Assembly, considering that ignorance, neglect, or contempt of human rights, are the sole causes of public misfortunes and corruptions of government, have resolved to set forth, in a solemn declaration, these natural, imprescriptible, and unalienable rights: that this declaration being constantly present to the minds of the members of the body social, they may be ever kept attentive to their rights and their duties: that the acts of the legislative and executive powers of government, being capable of being every moment compared with the end of political institutions, may be more respected: and also, that the future claims of the citizens, being directed by simple and incontestible principles, may always tend to the maintenance of the constitution, and the general happiness.

For these reasons, the NATIONAL ASSEMBLY doth recognize and declare, in the presence of the Supreme Being, and with the hope of his blessing and favour, the following *sacred* rights of men and of citizens:

I. *Men are born and always continue free, and equal in respect of their rights. Civil distinctions, therefore, can be founded only on public utility.*

II. *The end of all political associations is the preservation of the natural and imprescriptible rights of man; and these rights are—liberty, property, security, and resistance of oppression.*

III. *The nation is essentially the source of all sovereignty; nor can any expressly derived from it.*

IV. Political Liberty consists in the power of doing whatever does not injure another. The exercise of the natural rights of every man, has no other limits than those which are necessary to secure to every *other* man the free exercise of the same rights; and these limits are determinable only by the law.

V. The law ought to prohibit only actions hurtful to society. What is not prohibited by the law, should not be hindered; nor should anyone be compelled to that which the law does not require.

VI. The law is an expression of the will of the community. All citizens have a right to concur, either personally, or by their representatives, in its formation. It should be the same to all, whether it protects or punishes; and *all being equal in its sight, are equally eligible to all honours, places, and employments, according to their different abilities, without any other distinction than that created by their virtues and talents.*

VII. No man should be accused, arrested, or held in confinement, except in cases determined by the law, and according to the forms which it has prescribed. All who promote, solicit, execute, or cause to be executed, arbitrary orders, ought to be punished; and every citizen called upon or apprehended by virtue of the law, ought immediately to obey, and renders himself culpable by resistance.

VIII. The law ought to impose no other penalties than such as are absolutely and evidently necessary: and no one ought to be punished, but in virtue of a law promulgated before the offence, and legally applied.

IX. Every man being presumed innocent till he has been convicted, whenever his detention becomes indispensible, all rigour to him, more than is necessary to secure his person, ought to be provided against by the law.

X. No man ought to be molested on account of his opinions, not even on account of his *religious* opinions, provided his avowal of them does not disturb the public order established by the law.

XI. The unrestrained communication of thoughts and opinions being one of the most precious rights of man, every citizen may speak, write, and publish freely, provided he is responsible for the abuse of this liberty in cases determined by law.

XII. A public force being necessary to give security to the rights of men and of citizens, that force is instituted for the benefit of the community, and not for the particular benefit of the persons with whom it is entrusted.

XIII. A common contribution being necessary for the support of the public force, and for defraying the other expenses of government, it ought to be divided equally among the members of the community according to their abilities.

XIV. Every citizen has a right, either by himself or his representative, to a free voice in determining the necessity of public contributions, the appropriation of them, and their amount, mode of assessment, and duration.

XV. Every community has a right to demand of all its agents, an account of their conduct.

XVI. Every community in which a separation of power and a security of rights is not provided for, wants a constitution.

XVII. The right to property being inviolable and sacred, no one ought to be deprived of it, except in cases of evident public necessity legally ascertained, and on condition of a previous just indemnity.

THE RIGHTS OF MAN, DUBLIN, 1791

TO THE PEOPLE

A NORTHERN WHIG

Before I proceed to the object of this book, I think it necessary to acquaint the Reader, that I am a Protestant of the Church of Ireland, as by law established, and have again and again taken all the customary oaths by which we secure and appropriate to ourselves all degrees and professions, save one, to the utter exclusion of our Catholic Brethren. I am, therefore, no further interested in the event, than as a mere lover of justice, and a steady detester of tyranny, whether exerted by one man or one million.

The present state of Ireland is such, as is not to be paralleled in history or fable: Inferior to no country in Europe in the gifts of nature, blest with a temperate sky and a fruitful soil, intersected by many great rivers, indented round her whole coast with the noblest harbours, abounding with all the necessary materials for unlimited commerce, teeming with inexhaustible mines of the most useful metals, filled by 4,000,000 of an ingenious and a gallant people, with bold hearts, and ardent spirits; posted right in the track between Europe and America, within 50 miles

of England, 300 of France; yet with all these great advantages, unheard
of and unknown, without pride, or power, or name, without ambassa-
dors, army, or navy; not of half the consequence in the empire of which
she has the honour to make a part, with the single county of York, or the
loyal and well regulated town of Birmingham!

These are, or should be, to every true Irishman, mortifying considerations . . .

The proximate cause of our disgrace is our evil government, the
remote one is our own intestine division, which, if once removed, the
former will be instantaneously reformed . . .

The misfortune of Ireland is, that we have *no National Government*, in
which we differ from England, and from all Europe.

What is our Government? It is a phenomenon in politics, contraven-
ing all received and established opinions: It is a Government derived
from another country, whose interest, so far from being the same with
that of the people, directly crosses it at right angles: How is this foreign
Government maintained? Look to your court calendar, to your pension
list, to your concordatum, and you will find the answer written in *letters
of gold*: This unnatural influence must be supported by profligate means,
and hence corruption is the only medium of Government in Ireland.
The people is utterly disregarded and defied. Divided and distracted as
they are, and distrustful of each other, they fall an easy prey to English
rulers, or their Irish subalterns . . .

We see all this at the very hour, when everywhere but in Ireland
Reform is going forward, and levelling
ancient abuses in the dust. Why are these
things so? Because Ireland is struck with a
political paralysis, that has withered her
strength, and crushed her spirit: She is not half
alive, one side is scarce animated, the other is
dead; she has by her own law, as it were,
amputated her right hand; she has outrun the
Gospel precept, and cast her right eye into the
fire, even before it has offended her: Religious
intolerance and political bigotry, like the tyrant Mezentius, bind the living Protestant to
the dead and half corrupted Catholic, and
beneath the putrid mass, even the embryo of
effort is stifled . . .

My argument is simply this: That Ireland,

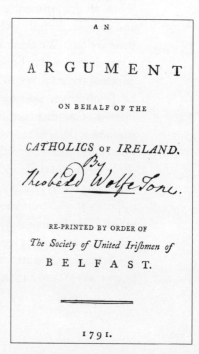

AN

ARGUMENT

ON BEHALF OF THE

CATHOLICS OF *IRELAND*.

By
Theobald Wolfe Tone.

RE-PRINTED BY ORDER OF
The Society of United Irishmen of
BELFAST.

1791.

as deriving her government from another country, requires a strength in the people, which may enable them, if necessary, to counteract the influence of that government, should it ever be, as it indisputably has been, exerted, to thwart her prosperity: That this strength may be most constitutionally acquired, and safely and peaceably exerted through the medium of a Parliamentary Reform: And finally, that no Reform is honourable, practicable, efficacious or just, which does not include as a fundamental principle, the extension of elective franchise to the Roman Catholics.

AN ARGUMENT ON BEHALF OF THE CATHOLICS OF IRELAND, BELFAST, 1791

DECLARATION AND RESOLUTIONS OF THE SOCIETY OF UNITED IRISHMEN OF BELFAST

In the present great era of reform, when unjust governments are falling in every quarter of Europe; when religious persecution is compelled to abjure her tyranny over conscience; when the rights of man are ascertained in theory, and that theory substantiated by practice; when antiquity can no longer defend absurd and oppressive forms, against the common sense and common interests of mankind; when all government is acknowledged to originate from the people, and to be so far only obligatory as it protects their rights and promotes their welfare: We think it our duty, as Irishmen, to come forward, and state what we feel to be our heavy grievance, and what we know to be its effectual remedy. WE HAVE NO NATIONAL GOVERNMENT; we are ruled by Englishmen, and the servants of Englishmen, whose object is the interest of another country, whose instrument is corruption, and whose strength is the weakness of Ireland; and these men have the whole of the power and patronage of the country, as means to seduce and to subdue the honesty and the spirit of her representatives in the legislature. Such an extrinsic power, acting with uniform force in a direction too frequently opposite to the true line of our obvious interests, can be resisted with effect solely by *unanimity, decision, and spirit in the people*; qualities which may be exerted most legally, constitutionally, and efficaciously, by that great measure essential to the prosperity and freedom of Ireland. AN EQUAL REPRESENTATION OF ALL THE PEOPLE IN PARLIAMENT. We do not here mention as grievances, the rejection of a place-bill, of a pension-bill, of a responsibility-bill, the sale of Peerages in one House, the corruption publicly avowed in the other, nor the notorious infamy of borough traffic between both; not that we are insensible of their enormity, but that we consider them as but symptoms of that mortal disease which corrodes the vitals of our Constitution, and leaves to the people, in their own Government, but the shadow of a name.

Impressed with these sentiments, we have agreed to form an association, to be called 'THE SOCIETY OF UNITED IRISHMEN:' And we do pledge ourselves to our country, and mutually to each other, that we will steadily support, and endeavor, by all due means, to carry into effect, the following resolutions:

> First, Resolved, That the weight of English influence in the Government of this country is so great, as to require a cordial union among ALL THE PEOPLE OF IRELAND, to maintain that balance which is essential to the preservation of our liberties, and the extension of our commerce.
>
> Second, That the sole constitutional mode by which this influence can be opposed, is by a complete and radical reform of the representation of the people in Parliament.
>
> Third, That no reform is practicable, efficacious, or just, which shall not include Irishmen of every *religious* persuasion.

Satisfied, as we are, that the intestine divisions among Irishmen have too often given encouragement and impunity to profligate, audacious, and corrupt Administrations, in measures which, but for these divisions, they durst not have attempted; we submit our resolutions to the nation, as the basis of our political faith.

We have now gone to what we conceive to be the remedy. With a Parliament thus reformed, every thing is easy; without it, nothing can be done: and we do call on and most earnestly exhort our countrymen in general to follow our example, and to form similar societies in every quarter of the kingdom, for the promotion of constitutional knowledge, the abolition of bigotry in religion and politics, and the equal distribution of the rights of man through all sects and denominations of Irishmen. The people, when thus collected, will feel their own weight, and secure that power which theory has already admitted as their portion, and to which, if they be not aroused by their present provocations to vindicate it, they deserve to forfeit their pretensions FOR EVER.

THEOBALD WOLFE TONE, BELFAST, OCTOBER 1791

At a meeting of the Society of United Irishmen of Dublin,
the Hon. Simon Butler in the chair, the following was agreed to:

When we reflect how often the freemen and freeholders of Dublin have been convened, humbly to express their grievances to Parliament; how often they have solicited the enaction of good, and the repeal of bad laws; how often, for successive years, they have petitioned against the obnoxious and unconstitutional Police Act; and how often all these applications have been treated with the most perfect contumacy and contempt—When these facts are brought to recollection, is there an honest man will say, that the House of Commons have the smallest respect for the people, or believe themselves their legitimate representatives. The fact is, that the great majority of that house, consider themselves as the representatives of their own money, or the hired servants of the English government;—whose minister here, is appointed for the sole purpose of dealing out corruption to them—at the expense of Irish liberty, Irish commerce, and Irish improvement.—This being the case, it naturally follows, that such minister is not only the representative of the English views against this country, but is also *the sole representative of the people of Ireland.* To elucidate which assertion, it is only necessary to ask, whether a single question in favour of this oppressed nation can be carried without his consent?—and whether any measure, however inimical, may not through his influence be effected?

In this state of abject slavery, no hope remains for us, but in the sincere and hearty *union of all the people*, for a complete and radical reform of

parliament; because it is obvious, that *one party alone* have been ever unable to obtain a single blessing for their country; and the policy of our rulers has been always such, as to keep the different sects at variance, in which they have been too well seconded by our own folly.

For the attainment then of this great and important object—for the removal of absurd and ruinous distinctions—and for promoting a complete coalition of the people—a club has been formed, composed of

JAMES NAPPER TANDY

all religious persuasions, who have adopted for their name,—the Society
of United Irishmen of Dublin—and have taken as their declaration that
of a similar society in Belfast.

JAMES NAPPER TANDY, SECRETARY,

BELFAST NEWS-LETTER, 16–20 DECEMBER 1791

Erin go Bragh!

JOHN BARR. fecit.

Green were the fields where my forefathers dwelt, O,
 Erin mavourneen, slan leat go-bragh!
Our farm it was small, yet comfort we felt, O,
 Erin mavourneen, slan leat go-bragh!
At length came the time when our lease did expire,
And fain would I live where before liv'd my sire,
But ah! well-a-day! I was forc'd to retire —
 Erin mavourneen, slan leat go-bragh!

Though all taxes I paid, yet no vote could I pass, O,
 Erin mavourneen, slan leat go-bragh!
I aggravated no great man, I feel it, alas, O,
 Erin mavourneen, slan leat go-bragh!
Forc'd from my home, yea, from where I was born,
To range the wide world, poor, helpless, forlorn,
I look back with regret, and my heart-strings are torn
 Erin mavourneen, slan leat go-bragh!

With princely a pure, patriotic, and firm,
 Erin mavourneen, slan leat go-bragh!
Attach'd to my country, a friend to reform,
 Erin mavourneen, slan leat go-bragh!
I supported old Ireland—was ready to die for't—
If her foes e'er prevail'd, I was well known to sigh for't—
But my faith I preserv'd, and am now forc'd to fly for't—
 Erin mavourneen, slan leat go-bragh!

But, hark! I hear sounds, and my heart strong is beating!
 Erin mavourneen, slan leat go-bragh!
Friendship advancing, delusion retreating!
 Erin mavourneen, slan leat go-bragh!
We've numbers, and numbers do constitute power,
Let's will to be free, and we're free from that hour;
Of Hibernia's sons, yes! we'll then be the flower—
 Erin mavourneen, slan leat go-bragh!

In the North I see friends, too long I've so-a blind, O!
 Erin mavourneen, slan leat go-bragh!
The cobweb is woken, and free is my mind, O!
 Bouldoch mavourneen, Erin go-bragh!
North and south here's my hand, and and here's my heart, O!
Let's ne'er be divided by any base art, O!
But love one another, and never more part, O!
 B-oldoch mavourneen, Erin go-bragh!

Too long we have suffer'd, and too long lamented,
 Bouldoch mavourneen, Erin go-bragh!
By courage undaunted, it may be prevented,
 Bouldoch mavourneen, Erin go-bragh!
No more by oppression let us be derided,
But with heart and hand, let's be firmly united,
For by Erin go-bragh it is thus we're to-be bind,
 Bouldoch mavourneen, Erin go-bragh!

——Belfast—Printed at the public Printing Office, 115, High-street, where may be had a great Variety of Ballads, Pictures, Pamphlets, &c. &c.

1792–1794

NO FEAR BUT THAT OF FORFEITURE

WILLIAM TODD JONES

Understanding that a solicitude respecting the security of Protestant tenures, should the Roman Catholics be restored to their parliamentary privileges, has lately a good deal agitated some liberal-minded men in Ulster; a solicitude much increased by a general persuasion that a map now secretly exists, delineating the districts and manors of each forfeiting family—I take the liberty of addressing to so meretorious an Association, a few pages regarding an *apprehension* which appears to me unfounded and delusive; and powerfully subversive of the present auspicious and progressive interests of this late emerging country. And I remember that upon moving the Address to Lord Charlemont at Belfast, in behalf of the Catholics, in 1784, when a few supposed great authorities of the day were against us, and when we carried it by means of the people, in opposition to their leaders, the only argument I had to combat was the terror of forfeiture: the danger of the church was not mentioned, nor apprehended: and when circular letters were, in no very dignified manner secretly dispatched by expresses to Derry, and to other Volunteer Assemblies, afterwards to be reviewed, to defeat the progress of that munificent sentiment, no fear but that of forfeiture was inculcated—which underhand efforts of a few, successful for the time against the principles of the MANY, I recall to your recollection, to warn you against similar attempts and consequences in future.—Confide not in assumed authorities; the liberal and the moderate, *upon their own principles*, must be with you; and the *bigotted in this question*, however learned, or amiable, are to be pitied ! and—to be laid aside !—If they have aught substantial to offer, let them come forward with their names, and boldly combat and confute: for notwithstanding the defeat of that day, we persevered in maintaining, that before a lapse of a dozen years, the sentiment would gain ground;—that the argument of policy and justice would supercede the operations of avarice or of zeal; and your valuable Association, gentlemen, affords an honourable illustration how reasonably grounded was that opinion.

A LETTER TO THE SOCIETIES OF UNITED IRISHMEN OF THE TOWN OF BELFAST, DUBLIN, 1792

Liberality, taking philosophy for her guide, pervades the minds of men.—On the 23d inst. a society was formed in the town of Clonmel, consisting of twenty-six original members, of all religious persuasions, who, after a very long conference, resolved to the following purport:

ARCHIBALD HAMILTON ROWAN

First, That at this enlightened aera, it was the duty of every Irishman to exert his utmost ability and influence, to remove religious prejudices from the minds of the ignorant of all religious persuasions.

Secondly, That the representation in Parliament demanded a radical reform; it being at present partial, and acted upon by undue influence, and therefore, every means, consistent with the true principles of the constitution, should be adopted for the purpose of restoring to the people that weight in the legislature to which they were entitled.

Thirdly, That the society do, immediately, open a correspondence with the United Irishmen of Dublin, and of Belfast.

Fourthly, That on every night of meeting a ballot be opened for the admission of Members.

At this meeting Thomas Sadlier, Esq. was elected chairman, and Leonard M'Nally, Esq. acted as secretary for the night.

The following gentlemen were elected honorary Members:

The Hon. Simon Butler, Leonard M'Nally, Esq. Dominick Rice, Esq., Hamilton Rowan, Esq., Todd Jones, Esq., Theobald Wolfe Tone, Esq., Dr. M'Kenna, Dr. Burke, Mr. Simon Maguire, Mr. Rich. M'Cormick, secretary to the Roman Catholic Committee, and a few others.

BELFAST NEWS-LETTER, 30 MARCH – 3 APRIL 1792

CAPTURE OF THE FRENCH KING

DETHRONEMENT OF LOUIS XVI

THE KING OF THE FRENCH IS DETHRONED!

On Thursday night the Assembly proceeded to debate the question concerning the dethroning of the King. The populace, in the meantime, stirred up by the Jacobins, who had been defeated in the question concerning the accusation against M. La Fayette, had assembled in immense numbers, not only in the Galleries but round the Hall, and at the Thuilleries.

At the latter place they proceeded to the most daring outrages, calling out *no King—he is a traitor, and does everything in his power to betray the interests of the Nation.* From unbridled vociferation they proceeded to acts of violence, and attacked the Swiss guards with a view to enter the palace, for the avowed purpose of exterminating the Royal Family.

The King, apprised of his danger, contrived to make his escape from the palace, accompanied by the Queen and the Dauphin, and fairly entered the Assembly, as a sanctuary, before it was known which way he had gone.

The populace, enraged at the resistance of the Guards, proceeded to exercise upon such of them as fell into their hands the utmost acts of cruelty, hanging some, and cutting others in pieces.

The Assembly, weak and timid, were obliged to comply with the mad mandates of the people, and at ten o'clock at night, decreed the dethronement, the King sitting at the same time among them.

NORTHERN STAR, 15–18 AUGUST 1792

ADDRESS

FROM THE

SOCIETY OF UNITED IRISHMEN, IN DUBLIN,

TO THE

DELEGATES FOR PROMOTING A REFORM

IN SCOTLAND

WILLIAM DRENNAN,

CHAIRMAN

ARCHIBALD HAMILTON ROWAN,

SECRETARY

23 November 1792

We take the liberty of addressing you, in the spirit of civic union, in the fellowship of a just and common cause. We greatly rejoice that the spirit of freedom moves over the surface of Scotland; that light seems to break from the chaos of her internal government; and that a country so respectable for her attainments in science, in arts, and in arms; for men of literary eminence; for the intelligence and morality of her people, now acts from a conviction of the union between virtue, letters, and liberty; and, now rises to distinction, not by a calm, contented, secret wish for a Reform in Parliament, but by openly, actively, and urgently *willing* it, with the unity and energy of an embodied nation. We rejoice that you do not consider yourselves as merged and melted down into another country, but that in this great national question, you are still—Scotland—the land where Buchannan wrote, and Fletcher spoke, and Wallace fought.

BELFAST NEWS-LETTER, 30 NOVEMBER–4 DECEMBER 1792

THE CATHOLIC PETITION

THE HUMBLE PETITION OF THE UNDERSIGNED CATHOLICS, ON BEHALF OF THEMSELVES, AND THE REST OF THE CATHOLIC SUBJECTS OF THE KINGDOM OF IRELAND.

EDWARD BYRNE, JOHN KEOGH, JAMES EDWARD DEVEREUX, CHRISTOPHER BELLEW, AND

SIR THOMAS FRENCH

MOST GRACIOUS SOVEREIGN

We your Majesty's most dutiful and loyal Subjects of your Kingdom of Ireland, professing the Catholic Religion, presume to approach your Majesty, who are the common Father of all your People, and humbly to submit to your consideration, the manifold incapacities, and oppressive disqualifications, under which we labour.

For, may it please your Majesty, after a century of uninterrupted

loyalty, in which time, five foreign wars, and two domestic rebellions have occurred; after having taken every oath of allegiance and fidelity to your Majesty, and given, and being still ready to give every pledge, which can be devised for their peaceable demeanour, and unconditional submission to the laws; the Catholics of Ireland stand obnoxious to a long Catalogue of Statutes, inflicting on dutiful and meritorious subjects, pains and penalties, of an extent and severity, which scarce any degree of delinquency can warrant; and prolonged to a period when no necessity can be alleged to justify such continuance.

JOHN KEOGH

THE PETITION OF THE CATHOLICS OF IRELAND, DUBLIN, 1793

NATIONAL CONVENTION

Monday, December 31, 1792

The Minister for Foreign Affairs gave an account of the hostile preparations which were making in England, and the resolutions of the Executive Council in consequence. He requested that immediately after the Convention had decided on the fate of Louis Capet, four Commissioners might be appointed to visit the arsenals in the ports of *Toulon, Brest*, and *Rochefort*.

Various Petitions and Addresses were presented, chiefly relative to the pending Trial of the King, some demanding a speedy punishment, others desiring it might be delayed.

Several other matters underwent discussion, but they were not of importance to interest public curiosity.

TRIAL OF LOUIS CAPET

Vergniaud. — Citizens, in so important a question, which is so intimately related with the tranquility and the glory of the nation, it is necessary to distinguish passions from principles, or the impulsions of the soul from the measures of general safety. Permit me to represent to you a few ideas upon the Sovereignty of the People. What is the Sovereignty of the people? It is the power of making laws, or regulations; in short, all the acts which are interesting to the felicity of the social order: the People exercise that power either by themselves, or by their representatives. In the latter case, which is our's, the decisions of the Representatives are executed as laws . . .

The soldier Cymber entered in the prison of Marius with a design to kill him, but ran away, struck with his awful aspect; but had he been a Member of the Senate, do you think he would have hesitated a moment to vote for the death of the Tyrant. As many Members treated this subject politically, said Vergniaud, I shall likewise presume to speak politically. Perhaps several Powers, who have not yet declared war against us, have abstained from it for fear of hastening the catastrophe of Louis; England and Spain are, perhaps, only waiting for such a pretence, in order to join our numerous enemies . . .

The trial of Louis Capet was then resumed.

Petit.—The existence of Capet is the attractive center which favours every enemy to liberty and every common disturber. Doubtlessly the punishment of death is surprising, terrible: but what is death of two minutes compared to the lengthened and slow conspiracy of Louis, who would have chained a nation by the death of an hundred thousand French? Yes, the great and bloody shade of Louis shall run through all Europe, shall terrify every despot, and carry dread and dismay even to those iron souls who occupy a throne.

NORTHERN STAR, 9–12 JANUARY 1793

EXECUTION OF LOUIS XVI

Paris, Tuesday, January 22, 1793

Conformably to the arrangements made by the Executive council, *Louis* was yesterday put to death at the *Place de la Revolution*, heretofore *Place de Louis XV*.

Twenty-five citizens, of known principles, well armed, acquainted with the manual exercise, and having each sixteen rounds of shot, were chosen from each section to form a guard of twelve hundred men, who accompanied the unfortunate monarch to the place of execution.

Strong detachment from the different legions were posted in the streets through which the royal prisoner was to pass, and also in all the avenues leading to the *Place de la Revolution*, to prevent any confusion; and each section had a body in reserve, ready to move at a moment's notice, to maintain public order, should any attempts have been made to disturb it.

Cannon were also distributed in every quarter where it was thought they could be any way serviceable, had events made it necessary to employ them.

Between eight and nine o'clock in the morning *Louis* proceeded from his apartment in the Temple, and got into the Mayor's carriage, who accompanied him, as did also M. Edgworth, or de Fermon, an Irish Priest whom he requested might attend him. *Louis* was dressed in a brown greatcoat, white waistcoat, black breeches and stockings; his hair was dressed.

The procession, commanded by Mareschal Santerre, proceeded along the Boulevards to the *Place de la Revolution*. One hundred Gendarmes on horseback formed an advanced guard to the procession. The rear guard was composed of one hundred national guards from the military school, also mounted. Various reserves of cavalry lined the procession and patrolled the outskirts of the city.

Louis arrived at the foot of the Scaffold, at twenty minutes past ten. He mounted the Scaffold with firmness and dignity, he appeared desirous to address the people, but even this last wish was denied him, drums and trumpets gave the signal, and at twenty-two minutes past ten, his head was severed from his body.

The *Place de la Revolution* was so strongly guarded by troops, that no person was suffered to pass after the King had entered it.

After his death, the nearest spectators divided among them what of his hair had been cut off by the stroke of the guillotine! and several persons dipped their handkerchiefs in his blood, which they afterwards carried about, crying, "Behold the blood of a tyrant!"

When the executioners shewed his head to the people, cries of "*Vive la Nation! Vive la Republique!*" were heard on all sides, and several groups made use of the following expressions: "We always wished well to him, but he never wished well to us!" Many, however, shewed emotions of a different nature.

His body was transported to the parish church of *La Madalene*, where
it was interred without any insult being offered to it, between the
persons who lost their lives during the illuminations on account of his
marriage, and the Swiss who fell on the 10th of August.

Louis, before his departure from the Temple, delivered to the Commissioners of the Council General, who were upon guard, his latter-will;
two copies of which he had written on the 25th of December last.—A
copy of which I hope to send you tomorrow.

Three thousand livers (£120 sterling) were found in his apartments at
the Temple, which were sent to the Council General of the Commons.

The city remained quiet, in gloomy silence, through the whole of the
day, in the morning, the shops were shut, and no woman was allowed to
be in the streets till the procession had returned with the body of Louis.

NORTHERN STAR, 26–30 JANUARY 1793

LORD BAYHAM TO THE HONOURABLE
ROBERT STEWART

Berkeley Square, February 4, 1793

Dear Robert—I very little deserve the indulgence and the information you have given me, having neither acknowledged the
receipt of your two excellent letters, nor informed you of the
impression the state of your country makes in this. I am sorry to confess
my ideas upon the subject are very gloomy; and I have no conception, in
these times, when rights are pushed to the utmost extremity, and reform
knows no bounds, of giving to any nation, and less to one of the description of yours, whose characteristic is certainly not moderation, the sort
of latitude which the questions about to take place in Ireland will give
them. I inherit, and upon consideration am clearly of my father's
opinion, that Ireland must be our province, if she will not be persuaded
to a Union; and, if she would, she ought and would enjoy complete and
reciprocal benefits with this country. This is my opinion; but, in the
present state of politics there, it would be dangerous either to maintain
that opinion, or to act in consequence of it; and the desirable thing *at
present* is to quiet and to satisfy the minds of the moderate men.

MEMOIRS AND CORRESPONDENCE OF VISCOUNT CASTLEREAGH, 4 FEBRUARY 1793

The King's Message respecting the Declaration of War with France. Feb. 11. Mr. Secretary Dundas presented the following Message from his Majesty:

"George R.

"His Majesty thinks proper to acquaint the House of Commons, that the assembly now exercising the powers of government in France, have, without previous notice, directed acts of hostility to be committed against the persons and property of his majesty's subjects, in breach of the law of nations, and of the most positive stipulations of treaty, and have since, on the most groundless pretences, actually declared war against his majesty and the United Provinces. Under the circumstances of this wanton and unprovoked aggression, his majesty has taken the

necessary steps to maintain the honour of his crown, and to vindicate the rights of his people; and his majesty relies with confidence on the firm and effectual support of the House of Commons, and on the zealous exertions of a brave and loyal people, in prosecuting a just and necessary war, and in endeavouring, under the blessing of Providence, to oppose an effectual barrier to the farther progress of a system which strikes at the security and peace of all independent nations, and is pursued in open defiance of every

KING GEORGE III

principle of moderation, good faith, humanity, and justice.

"In a cause of such general concern, his majesty has every reason to hope for the cordial co-operation of those powers who are united with his majesty by the ties of alliance, or who feel an interest in preventing the extension of anarchy and confusion, and in contributing to the security and tranquillity of Europe.

"G.R."

Debate in the Commons on the King's Message respecting the Declaration of War with France.

HANSARD'S PARLIAMENTARY DEBATES, 11 FEBRUARY 1793

CATHOLIC RELIEF

Whereas various acts of parliament have been passed, imposing on his Majesty's subjects professing the popish or Roman catholic religion, many restraints and disabilities, to which other subjects of this realm are not liable; and from the peaceable and loyal demeanour of his Majesty's popish, or Roman Catholick subjects, it is fit that such restraints and disabilities shall be discontinued: Be it therefore enacted by the King's most excellent Majesty, by and with the advice and consent of the lords spiritual and temporal, and

GENERAL COMMITTEE
OF THE
CATHOLICS of IRELAND.
Taylors-Hall, Back-Lane.
TUESDAY, APRIL 16, 1793.

commons in this present parliament assembled, and by the authority of the same, That his Majesty's subjects being papists, or persons professing the popish or Roman catholick religion, or married to papists, or persons professing the popish or Roman catholick religion, or educating any of their children in that religion, shall not be liable or subject to any penalties, forfeitures, disabilities, or incapacities, or to any laws for the limitation, charging, or discovering of their estates and property, real or personal, or touching the acquiring of property, or securities affecting property, save such as his Majesty's subjects of the protestant religion are liable and subject to; and that such parts of all oaths as are required to be taken by persons in order to qualify themselves for voting at elections of members to serve in parliament; and also such parts of all oaths required to be taken by persons voting at elections for members to serve in parliament, as import to deny that the person taking the same is a papist or married to a papist, or educates his children in the popish religion, shall not hereafter be required to be taken by any voter, but shall be omitted by the person administering the same; and that it shall not be necessary, in order to entitle a papist, or person professing the popish or Roman catholick religion to vote at an election of members to serve in parliament, that he should at, or previous to his voting, take the oaths of allegiance and abjuration, any statute now in force, to the contrary of any of the said matters in any wise notwithstanding.

II. Provided always, and be it further enacted, That all papists, or persons professing the popish, or Roman catholick religion, who may claim to have a right of voting for members to serve in parliament, or of voting for magistrates in any city, town-corporate, or borough, within this kingdom, be hereby required to perform all qualifications, registries, and other requisites, which are now required of his Majesty's protestant subjects, in like cases, by any law or laws now of force in this kingdom, save and except such oaths and parts of oaths as are herein before excepted.

III. And provided always, That nothing herein before contained shall extend, or be construed to extend to repeal, or alter any law or act of parliament now in force, by which certain qualifications are required to be performed by persons enjoying any offices or places of trust under his Majesty, his heirs and successors, other than as herein after is enacted.

IV. Provided also, That nothing herein contained, shall extend, or be construed to extend, to give papists, or persons professing the popish religion, a right to vote at any parish vestry, for levying of money to rebuild or repair any parish church, or respecting the demising or disposal of the income of any estate belonging to any church or parish, or for the salary of the parish clerk, or at the election of any church warden.

v. Provided always, That nothing contained in this act, shall extend to, or be construed to affect any action, or suit now depending, which shall have been brought or instituted previous to the commencement of this session of parliament.

vi. Provided also, That nothing herein contained, shall extend to authorize any papist, or person professing the popish or Roman catholick religion, to have or keep in his hands or possession, any arms, armour, ammunition, or any warlike stores, sword-blades, barrels, locks, or stocks of guns, or firearms, or to exempt such person from any forfeiture, or penalty inflicted by any act respecting arms, armour, or ammunition, in the hands or possession of any papist, or respecting papists having or keeping such warlike stores, save and except papists, or persons of the popish or Roman catholick religion, seized of a freehold estate of one hundred pounds a year, or possessed of a personal estate of one thousand pounds or upwards, who are hereby authorized to keep arms and ammunition as Protestants now by law may; and also save and except papists or Roman catholicks, possessing a freehold estate of ten pounds yearly value, and less than one hundred, or a personal estate of three hundred, and less than one thousand pounds, who shall have at the session of the peace in the county in which they reside, taken the oath of allegiance prescribed to be taken by an act passed in the thirteenth and fourteenth years of his present Majesty's reign, entitled, *An act to enable his Majesty's subjects, of whatever persuasion, to testify their allegiance to him*; and also in open court, swear and subscribe an affidavit, that they are possessed of a freehold estate, yielding a clear yearly profit to the person making the same, of ten pounds, or a personal property of three hundred pounds above his just debts, specifying therein the name and nature of such freehold, and nature of such personal property, which affidavits shall be carefully preserved by the clerk of the peace, who shall have for his trouble a fee of six pence, and no more, for every such affidavit; and the person making such affidavits, and possessing such property, may keep and use arms and ammunition as protestants may, so long as they shall respectively possess a property of the annual value of ten pounds, and upwards, if freehold, or the value of three hundred pounds

AN ACT FOR THE RELIEF OF HIS MAJESTY'S POPISH OR
ROMAN CATHOLIC SUBJECTS OF IRELAND

DUBLIN, 1793

THOMAS RUSSELL

IT WILL END IN REPUBLICANISM

Thursday 4[th] of April [1793]. Set out for Dublin. Ar[r]ive in 3 days. The French disasters, the strong gover[n]ment, etc., etc., has almost extinguish'd spirit. The Catholicks to meet in general committee on the 16[th]. No hopes entertain'd. All despond. The north will emigrate in astonishing numbers so soon as they hear of the defection of the Catholicks. It is to be observed that the Catholick bill and the news of Dumourie[z]'s defection came over in the same paquet. America look'd on now as the only asylum as reform is out of the question. Neilson. Magog. Mr Hutton and I dined together and—tempora mutantur—could scarce keep each other awake.

[16–24 April 1793]. The Catholicks meet. At first very bad. Mend. Rubbing together gives them spirit. Their addresses stiff. Refuse to grant Hobart a service of plate which was moved for. Vote Mr Hutton £1500 inclusive of £200 received and 30 sprugs for a gold medal, £1000 to Todd Jones with a contingent £500 if they have it, £500 to Simon Butler, £100 for a piece of plate to Sam Neilson and £100 to buy books of Dr Dickson's. Good. The day before it was in contemplation to sell the *Northern Star* to gover[n]ment. I leave town the day they are to debate whether they will declare for reform. If that is carried all will go well. If not, America ho!

Wednesday, 24 [April 1793]. Set off for En[n]iskilling. A mix'd company. Such lies! The secret committee saved Ireland. 500 men assembled in Belfast. Gen[eral] White gave them only $1/2$ an hour to disperse and in the meantime prepared his forges and red hot balls to burn the town. A brother-in-law of Grattan's, a clergyman of the name of Elliot, says that Grattan sayd the United Irishmen had ruined the opposition. Says Grattan, "that cursed Society of United Irishmen have ruined opposition, render'd them quite unpopular and prevented their going the lengths *they otherwise would have done*". Heartily glad! If the club has done that, it has served the country by exposing that vile, ped[d]ling, pitiful faction.

[*Some days later*]. Hear from Tone that the xx [*Catholics*] have declared in the most decided manner for reform. This is good. Quere—will it procure it? I believe not. The spirit of the people is broken at present. The procrastination of the xx [*Catholic*] bill was a very wise measure of gover[n]ment. They waited for events and it answer'd. They had time to attack the spirited Protestants and that head of liberty—Belfast—and show their weakness to pull down the freedom of the press, etc., etc. All this time the xx [*Catholics*] were with their hands tied up. Now the tyranny of gover[n]men[t] is establish'd by precedent and who will dare begin to resist it? Two wise patriots, Mr Hutton and P.P., foresaw this. Had their advice been follow'd, it would not have been thus. We had our day and let it pass. Will it ever return in our time? What can put us up again? I see nothing but the continuance of the present ruinous war. Calamitous enough. I shall know more, however, when I go to Belfuscu. The gentry of Fermanagh horrible torys. This, however, rather from their being old, good *Protestants*. This will go off. P.P.'s women under a bad report. Confidently sayd that they are bloody politicians. Praise Payne. The day of the fast, whenever the king was pray'd for, stand up. Drink the fate of Louis to all crown'd heads, George the last, etc., etc. Good Lord! What abominable credulity and folly! Settle the women. Prepare to go to Belfuscu.

Monday, May 6th [1793]. Walking with Stack. Receive a summons sign'd Farnham from the lords' committee. The man who gives it the postmaster of Enniskillen. Says he was order'd by the peer who sign'd it to deliver it into my hand. How the devil did they trace me out? Dublin, ho!

Teusday 7 [May 1793]. Set out on foot by the way of Tempo . . . It has long been an hypothesis of mine, but I don't know if I committed it to writing, that this war would [be] long, bloody, general and almost the last with which Europe would be infested and that it would end in republicanism very generally. This I thought long before England engaged in the war. I write it down now to see how the event will answer. The late defeats of the French seem to make against it. Proccedeamus ...

10 [May 1793]. Mr Hutton arrives in town to see P.P. previous to his examination. P.P. examine[d]. Will not swear to other people's opinions nor answer such questions as would tend to criminate himself. The lords' committee evidently rascals, stupid, unfair and either ill-inform'd or pretending to be so. Ask opinions as to the French, volunteering, etc., etc., all of which are answer'd in such a manner as could not be pleasing to them. Don't show the alleg'd letter of Mr Hutton's to P.P. Won't pay P.P. his expenses. Sad doges! To the club at night. An amulet. Fight it off. Fools! The club declining, not above 40 present.

[Later]. In the country with Mr H[utton]. Think of what is to be done. Mr H[utton] is willing, if the [United Irishmen?] be willing, to risque all he has [to] go to an unanointed republic via London, etc., etc. P.P. coincides. Come to town. Consult Magog. He falls into it. P.P. sets off having raised the wind by virtue of Mr H[utton]'s time piece.

Arrive at Belfuscu. Sunday 19 [May 1793]. See McCabe and Neilson. Conversation. The spirit of the north as high and perhaps higher at this moment than at any other period, to witt Derry, Tyrone, Antrim, Down and part of Ardmagh, burning with indignation against gover[n]ment. They say they have gone the greatest lengths [to] hold out their hands to the nation to join them in the reform but they have refused. They have lately seen them insulted, etc., etc. From all this they conclude the sense of the country is against them. They, if they had the power, have not the right to force any question on their countrymen. This has always been their principle. Now they stand fast. They feel disgusted at the conduct of Ireland. They have been left alone and they will give themselves no further trouble, nor will [they] ever act in any manner *whatever* till their countrymen see their error and call on them. At the time they were making the greatest exertions the southern papers were abusing them. They are determined never to act in the slightest degree. The expression not a man in the town would put his feet where his toe was on any public account. The active men through the country, captain[s] of corps, etc., etc., all emigrating. Most of the town would [do so] if they could sell their property, which oweing to the fall of credit cannot now be done. This being the case, is not Ireland desperat[e]? 'Tis melancholy. They are not to be blamed. Yet I don't despair. The spirited people will be keep'd for a while in the country and things may come round. A slender hope. Poor Ireland! P.P. has ruined himself in the pursuit of the good of his country.

JOURNALS OF THOMAS RUSSELL, 4 APRIL – 19 MAY 1793

THE STATE OF THE COUNTRY

Major-General Crosbie set out yesterday morning to take the command of the troops in the province of Connaught.

Letters received yesterday in town from Enniskillen, state, that a rencontre took place in that quarter on Tuesday, between a party of rioters, amounting to some thousands, assembled to oppose the magistrates of the county, in carrying into effect the militia act, and a party of dragoons, in which seven of the former were killed, eleven wounded, and above one hundred taken prisoners.

We hear that a great mob of rioters assembled at Boyle, in the county of Roscommon, and were proceeding to commit outrages, till prevented by the military quartered in that town, who were obliged to fire upon them, whereby nineteen of them were killed, and several taken prisoners; amongst the latter was a gentleman of family, who having run through his fortune, had joined and headed these misguided people.

At Manor Hamilton, in the county of Leitrim, a like disturbance arose; a mob set upon an officer going through the town with a small party of the military, who were forced to fire in defence of their own lives—Eight of the rioters were killed and several wounded, when the rest took to flight.

NORTHERN STAR, 29 MAY – 1 JUNE 1793

THE SOCIETY OF UNITED IRISHMEN
TO THE
HON. SIMON BUTLER AND OLIVER BOND, ESQR.

GENTLEMEN—OUR DEAR AND RESPECTED FRIENDS!

On the first of March we saw you enter into prison with an air and manner that testified not only a serene and settled conviction in the justice of your cause, but a chearful confidence in your own fortitude to sustain all the consequences that an attachment to this cause might bring upon you . . .

Notwithstanding the irresistible argument of six months' imprisonment in a common gaol, we are still inclined to lament, that the law and the custom of Parliament should have ever entered into a contest with the liberty of the press and the rights of the people; and that a discretionary power of punishment should so often supercede the ordinary course of criminal jurisdiction and the sacred trial by jury.

BELFAST NEWS-LETTER, 23–27 AUGUST 1793

VAST MAJORITY WOULD JOIN THE FRENCH

Dublin on Sunday the 1[st] of Dec[embe]r [1793]. Call on Magog. Dine at the Tha[t]ch'd House in Castle St[reet]. The master, McCullough, the best singer I ever *heard*. To Mr Hutton at his seat in the country.

On Monday [2 December 1793] return to town.

On Teusday the famous 3rd of December dine at Magog's. Find that nothing in a political way is doing. All talking. See Rowan, Reynolds, etc., etc., who want to pursue some plan of making the country sensible of the benefits which would accrue from reform. Hamilton sett[l]es his business.

[*Date not stated*]. Return to Tone's. Dine with Griffith, a good, sensible man, and with Wogan Brown[e], who reads an essay on universal representation . . .

His theory of politicks is very ration[a]l for a man of fortune. To witt I or persons in my situation of life cannot be better'd by any political change, *but* the great majority of the people would be *benefitted* essentially, and if measures are not taken by the ruling people for their advantage they will [in the] end take the matter into their own hands and then woe to their oppressors and to the rich. The example of France will be followed and perhaps exceeded, and therefore it is that a man should sacrifice a part to preserve the remains. I wonder no people of fortune consider this, but on the contrary they wink hard to avoid seeing the gulph on the brink of which they tread and go on flattering themselves that France will be crush'd and its example not follow'd. Fatal delusion!

Tone and I go to Dublin in consequence of a letter from Rowan. Try to form a club to bring up the south to reform by writing and distribution. Mentions for it Magog, Reynoulds, Emmet, Sweetman (John), Rowan, Hutton and P.P. Gog mooted. Magog won't consort with him as he is a traytor. Call on Gog. Mr H[utton] and P.P. endeavour to get a dinner on foot to ballance *Moira's*. Gog eager for it and offers to do anything. Sees his popularity gone. The 2nd of January mention'd, on which day the king received the petition. Gog wants the opposition at it. Mr H[utton] doubts. P.P. strong against it. Call on Magog. He

THE UNFORTUNATE MARIE ANTOINETTE, LATE QUEEN OF FRANCE, GUILLOTINED 11 OCTOBER 1793

peremptorily refuses to dine on that day, as the cause of Ireland was lost in England by the delegates, and [he] says the citizens would not do it. Speak to Dr Ryan. He not averse to showing the spirit but does not like the day. *Drops* that dinner was a most *unfortunate event*, they should have another and the opposition to it is bad. Everything goes on from bad to worse. The French establishing their liberty will free us in our own *despight*. Down to the Chateau Boue. Mr Hutton determines to go to the bar. Glad at it. To Dublin. French driving all before them at Landau, etc., etc.

Return with Mr H[utton] and family to Dublin on Wedensday the 15 Janua[r]y [1794]. Find Hamilton is out of the army.

Friday [17 January 1794]. Sweetman (E.) dines with Mr H[utton]. Pleasant. His county, i.e. the lower orders, all alive and would do anything. Find I am ele[c]ted to the librarianship at Belfast, which Mr H[utton] and Stokes have put me out of conceit with. Mr H[utton] recommends matrimony.

Saturday [18 January 1794]. Set off for Enniskillen. Mr H[utton] and P.P. low enough. Mr H[utton] abuses the leaving [of] Dungannon, etc., etc. Walks to the end of the park. Will have it that the north are cowards and braggadocias and nothing to be expected from this country except from *sans culottes* who are too ignorant for any thinking man to wish to see in power. I think nothing can hinder a revolution in this country, but it may be sooner or later. It must be in 4 or 5 years. Part. Fall in with a boy between Dublin and Dunshauchling. He says the people in the county of Monaghan are in favor of the French. Says there are Defenders there. 300 armed. All for the French. That letters have come from France. That these people are fond of Fay who is in prison but that he knows nothing of them. Rescue. Ne plus ultra. Mr Mears O'Neil. Cha[i]se. McLoughlin. To Navan.

Sunday 19 [January 1794]. To Cavan, to the Miller. He in great joy. All come round. The speech of Roberspeir in favor of religion of great use. Vast majority in favor of the French. In the mounta[i]ns between Cavan and Baillybourou. Inhabited by xx [*Catholics*]. Wealthy. Grazing and corn. Have schools in the mountains. Their children taught Latton, etc., etc. All for the French. It was Sunday night when I went in. His little daughter reading the Douay Bible, they being xx [*Catholics*]. Vast majority would join the French.

SIR J.B. WARREN'S ACTION OFF IRELAND WITH A SQUADRON OF FRENCH FRIGATES

THE HOPES OF FRANCE UTTERLY DISAPPOINTED

Then Mr. *Speaker* reported, That the House had attended his Excellency the Lord Lieutenant in the House of Peers, where his Excellency was pleased to make a Speech to both Houses of Parliament, of which Mr. *Speaker* said, to prevent Mistakes, he had obtained a Copy, which he read to the House, and the same was afterwards read by the Clerk at the Table, and is as follows:

"My Lords and Gentlemen,

"I HAVE his Majesty's Commands to meet you in Parliament.

"You must have felt with the highest Satisfaction, that by the Success of his Majesty's Arms and those of his Allies, the Hopes of *France*, in the unprovoked Declaration of War, to impair the Stability or shake the Constitution of *Great Britain* and *Ireland*, have been utterly disappointed.

"The Forces of his Majesty and his Allies are in Possession of many important Fortresses which belonged to the *French*, and many of their oppressive and unjust Conquests have been wrested from them; and whilst the Trade of the Empire has been generall protected, the Resources which our Enemies derived from their wealthy Settlements and extensive Commerce have been almost entirely cut off.

"I have the Satisfaction to acquaint you that the Spirit of Insurrection which was for some Time prevalent among the lower Orders of the People is in general suppressed. No Exertion shall be wanting on my Part to bring them to a due Sense of Order and Subordination, and to prevent and punish the Machinations of those who may aim to seduce them from their accustomed Loyalty into Acts of Sedition and Outrage.

"The Law for rendering a Militia in this Kingdom effectual has been carried successfully into Execution; and I am happy to find that the People are at length fully reconciled to this Institution, which has already been attended by the most beneficial Consequences, in producing internal Tranquillity, and contributing to the general Strength and Force of the Empire.

"I am commanded to acquaint you that his Majesty has appointed a Commission under the Great Seal to execute the Office of Lord High Treasurer of this Kingdom, in order that the Payment of the Civil List granted to his Majesty, and a regular Appropriation of the Revenue to distinct Services, may be carried into Execution in a Manner as conformable to the Practice of *Great Britain* as the relative Situation of this Kingdom will permit."

JOURNALS OF THE HOUSE OF COMMONS, IRELAND, 9 JANUARY 1794

MR HAMILTON ROWAN

No man in any situation, in any station of life, ever experienced such unremitting virulence as Mr. HAMILTON ROWAN; for years past, in every proclamation print has that gentleman been branded with every crime that could disgrace him as a man, or outrage society. Mr. ROWAN, in the Castle prints, has invariably been represented as the life and soul—nay the very prop and treasury of the Defenders.

Was there a rumour of a plot, was there a conspiracy among the Catholics, was there a rebellion in Ulster, where the respectable, independent, and enlightened inhabitants of Belfast, exerting their influence, opening their arms to receive to Liberty and Equality, in the constitution, their fellow subjects, fellow natives of the land:

HAMILTON ROWAN—HAMILTON ROWAN—was the innovator, was the traitor, the disturber, the defender, the sole cause of the destruction of all credit; he that burst the bonds of society, he that dissolved all confidence between citizens. The National Bank refused all discounts—why? HAMILTON ROWAN—HAMILTON ROWAN—was the author, agitator, sole and only cause. Yet when all these charges were investigated,

when every exertion had been used by administration, and those in the
employ and confidence of that administration, after 15 months of preparation, and that aided by every exertion of ability at the bar, or ingenuity in the agents of every class, whether of the council, the cabinet, or the low informer; HAMILTON ROWAN is found guilty by a Jury— of what?—distributing an Address of the UNITED IRISHMEN.

NORTHERN STAR, 30 JANUARY–3 FEBRUARY 1794

PLAN FOR MORE COMPLETELY PROVIDING FOR THE SECURITY OF THE COUNTRY

March 26, 1794

Mr. Secretary Dundas presented the following Plan for Providing more Completely for the Security of the Country. Dated Whitehall. March 14, 1794.

In order to provide more completely for the security of the country against any attempts which may be made on the part of the enemy, it may be expedient to adopt some, or all, of the following measures:

1. To augment the militia by volunteer companies, as was practised in the last war; or by an additional number of volunteers, to be added as privates to each company.

2. To form volunteer companies in particular towns, especially in those situated on or near the sea coast, for the purpose of the local defence of the particular places where they may be raised, according to the accompanying plan, or such other as may, on application for that purpose, be approved of, as best adapted to the circumstances of any particular town.

3. To raise volunteer troops of fencible cavalry, consisting of not less than fifty, nor more than eighty, per troop; who will be to serve only during the war, and within the kingdom. The officers will have temporary rank only, and will not be entitled to half-pay: the arms, accoutrements, and clothing will be furnished by government; but the levy-money for the men to be furnished by the persons who undertake to raise such troops; and the horses to be found by them, but to be paid for, at a reasonable price, by government.—A person raising two troops, to have the temporary

rank of major; four troops, that of lieutenant colonel; and six troops that of colonel.

4. To form other bodies of cavalry within particular counties or districts, to consist of the gentlemen and yeomanry, or such persons as they shall bring forward, according to the plans to be approved of by the king, or by the lords lieutenants under authority from his majesty; and the officers to receive temporary commissions from his majesty, and the muster-rolls also to be approved by his majesty, or by the lords lieutenants, at the periods to be fixed. No levy-money to be given, and the horses to be furnished by the gentry or yeomanry who compose the corps, but the arms and accoutrements to be supplied at the expense of the public. Such corps to be exercised only at such times as shall be fixed by warrant from his majesty, or by the approbation of the lords lieutenants. To be liable to be embodied, or called out of their counties by special directions from his majesty, in case of actual appearance of invasion; and to be liable to be called upon, by order from his majesty, or by the lord lieutenant or sheriff of the county to act within the county, or in the adjacent counties, for the suppression of riots and tumults. In either case, while actually in service, they shall receive pay as cavalry, and be liable to the provisions of the mutiny bill.

HANSARD'S PARLIAMENTARY DEBATES, 26 MARCH 1794

THE KING AGAINST M'CABE AND OTHERS, PUBLISHERS AND PROPRIETORS OF A NEWSPAPER CALLED, *NORTHERN STAR*

This was an information *ex officio*, filed by the Attorney General against William M'Cabe, William Tennent, William Magee, R. Callwell, John Boyle, John Haslet, Henry Haslet, Samuel Nelson, Robert Simms, William Simms, Gilbert M'Ilveen, John Tisdall, as the proprietors of the said Newspaper, and John Rabb, as printer and publisher thereof—in which, on the 15th of December, 1792, false, scandalous, and seditious libel was published to the following effect:—

"That there existed no National Government in Ireland; that Parliament was controlled by British Influence, and was not a Representation of the People in that a majority of the House of Commons was returned by NINETY individuals; that nothing but a Radical Reform of the Parliament, by imparting the Elective Franchise to the great body of the People, could save this kingdom, and to effect it the inhabitants of England, Scotland, and Ireland were invited to turn their thoughts towards a Convention; that the Roman Catholics of this country were reduced below the state of African slaves, to the reproach of a Constitution falsely called free; that this libel purported to be an Address from the Jacobins of Belfast to the People, and they called upon the God of Nature to renounce them, if ever they desisted from their pursuits, &c." with intent to excite sedition and tumult amongst his Majesty's subjects . . ."

His Lordship declared that the libel in question was the most mischievous, seditious, and flagitious production he ever had the misfortune to read. It was impossible for a child to mistake its object, and the defendant, instead of shewing any thing like contrition for his conduct, had added impudence to guilt, and not only avowed, but gloried in his guilt.

Mr. Justice Downes perfectly concurred with Lord Clonmell—and the Jury after retiring for a short time, returned with a verdict—GUILTY.

At ten at night the Court adjourned.

Mr. Rabb was not in custody—he stands out on his recognizance.

BELFAST NEWS-LETTER, 30 MAY–2 JUNE 1794

ARRANGEMENTS IN IRELAND

We understand that the business of the Lord Lieutenancy, and the expected changes in the Ministers, and the measures of Ireland, still remain in that state of doubt and confusion, which we, a few days past, mentioned to have taken place immediately subsequent to the arrival of Mr. Beresford in this country.

Mr. Pitt still perseveres in protecting the Old Administration, at the head of which must be considered Lord Fitzgibbon, the Chancellor. While on the other hand, Lord Fitzwilliam, it is said, is equally positive

52   in refusing the Office of Lord Lieutenant, unless he can obtain the aid of Messrs. Grattan, Forbes, Ponsonby, and their Friends, whose *sine qua non* is the dismissal of the present Placemen, and the full adoption of the measures for which the present Minority have so long in vain struggled in that country.

BELFAST NEWS-LETTER, 27–31 OCTOBER 1794

CATHOLIC CONGRATULATION

1795–1797

PROTESTANT DISSENTERS' ADDRESS

On Monday last the Protestant Dissenters waited on his Excellency the Lord Lieutenant with the following Address:

To his Excellency William Fitzwilliam, Earl Fitzwilliam, Lord Lieutenant General, and General Governor of Ireland.

May it please your Excellency,

We beg leave, in the name, and by the appointment of his Majesty's dutiful and loyal subjects, the Protestant Dissenters of Ireland, to present our sincere congratulations to your Excellency, on your safe arrival in this kingdom. While we approach your Excellency with peculiar satisfaction, as the approved friend of civil and religious liberty, and the inheritor of the virtues of your illustrious kinsman, the late Marquis of Rockingham, we cannot but deem your Excellency's appointment to the high station you now hold, a distinguished mark of his Majesty's paternal regard for the interests of this country.

Deriving from our ancestors a high and sacred veneration for the principles of the glorious revolution, which placed the august house of Hanover on the Throne of these kingdoms, we humbly trust that our conduct will on every occasion secure your Excellency's favourable representation of our affectionate and steady attachment to the person, family and government of our most gracious Sovereign.

Permit us to express our conviction that your Excellency's administration will be directed by that enlightened wisdom which cannot fail to promote the true dignity of his Majesty's Crown, and your Excellency's highest honour, as inseparable from the real welfare, prosperity and happiness of Ireland.

NORTHERN STAR, 15–19 JANUARY 1795

ROMAN CATHOLIC EMANCIPATION

Mr. Grattan said there was another subject he had to mention to the House, which was, that he should move for leave to bring in a bill for the further relief of his Majesty's subjects of this kingdom professing *the Roman Catholic religion*. In this he should proceed as was done in the session of 1793, when the business was taken up, in the first instance, by way of bill. If he should get leave to bring in the bill, his intention was to give gentlemen time to give it consideration.—He then moved for leave to bring in the bill.

Dr. Duignan hoped the Right Hon. Gentleman did not intend to precipitate business of this very momentous nature. It was a measure of the greatest moment. He considered it a momentous and gigantic measure, and he hoped that the consideration of it would be postponed till after the assizes. He again entreated of the Right Hon. Gentleman not to precipitate this business, but that sufficient time would be allowed to gentlemen to give this important subject the most serious consideration . . .

On the question being put that leave be given to bring in the bill, it was carried in the affirmative with only two dissenting voices, which we apprehend were Mr. Ogle and Mr. Duignan.

BELFAST NEWS-LETTER, 13–16 FEBRUARY 1795

THE EXILED
IRISHMAN'S LAMENTATION
Tune—"SAVOURNA DEILISH."

GREEN were the fields where my forefathers dwelt, O;
>   *Erin ma vorneen! slan leat go brah!* *
Although our farm it was small, yet comforts we felt O.
>   *Erin ma vorneen! slan leat go brah!*
At length came the day when our lease did expire,
And fain would I live where before liv'd my sire;
But, ah! well-a-day! I was forced to retire.
>   *Erin ma vorneen! slan leat go brah!*

Though all taxes I paid, yet no vote could I pass, O;
>   *Erin ma vorneen! slan leat go brah!*
Aggrandized no great man—and I feel it, alas! O;
>   *Erin ma vorneen! slan leat go brah!*
Forced from my home; yea, from where I was born,
To range the wide world—poor, helpless, forlorn;
I look back with regret—and my heart-strings are torn.
>   *Erin ma vorneen! slan leat go brah!*
With principles pure, patriotic and firm,
>   *Erin ma vorneen! slan leat go brah!*

To my country attached, and a friend to reform,
                            Erin ma vorneen! slan leat go brah!
I supported old Ireland—was ready to die for it;
If her *foes* e'er prevail'd, I was well known to sigh for it;
But my faith I preserved, and am now fore'd to fly for it.
                            Erin ma vorneen! slan leat go brah!

In the North I see friends—too long was I blind, O;
                            Erin ma vorneen! slan leat go brah!
The cobwebs are broken, and free is my mind, O.
                            Erin ma vorneen! slan leat go brah!
North and South here's my hand—East and West here's my heart, O;
Let's ne'er be divided by any base art, O;
But love one another, and never more part, O.
                            Boie yudh ma vorneen! Erin go brah!†

But hark! I hear sounds, and my heart strong is beating,
                            Boie yudh ma vorneen! Erin go brah!
Friendship advancing—delusion retreating.
                            Boie yudh ma vorneen! Erin go brah!
We have numbers—and numbers do constitute power:
Let's WILL TO BE FREE—and we're Free from that hour:
Of Hibernia's Sons—yes—we'll then be the flower.
                            Boie yudh ma vorneen! Erin go brah!

Too long have we suffer'd, and too long lamented:
                            Boie yudh ma vorneen! Erin go brah!
By courage undaunted it may be prevented.
                            Boie yudh ma vorneen! Erin go brah!
No more by oppressors let us be affrighted,
But with heart, and with hand, be firmly United;
For by *Erin go brah! 'tis thus will be righted.*
                            Boie yudh ma vorneen! Erin go brah!

* Ireland my darling! for ever adieu!
† Victory to you my darling! Ireland for ever!

PADDY'S RESOURCE, BELFAST, 1795

EARL FITZWILLIAM,
Late Lord Lieutenant of Ireland?

EARL FITZWILLIAM'S DEPARTURE

Yesterday will be remembered as the most ominous and fatal to the interests of Ireland that has occurred within the present century. At eleven o'clock his Excellency Earl Fitzwilliam held his last levee, which for brilliancy and numbers eclipsed anything of the sort which we recollect to have seen at St. James's. His Excellency continued about an hour and a half in the room, receiving the cordial compliments of the true friends of the nation for his patriotic intentions, with an affability and manner peculiarly his own. Never, perhaps, was there more unaffected sincerity beheld at any Court. If the melancholy occasion did not afford the feast of reason, it at least called forth the flow of soul.

NORTHERN STAR, 26–30 MARCH 1795

The partizans of the English Ministry affect to deny that the British Cabinet have any thoughts of proposing an UNION. They find it so unpalatable to the bulk of this nation, whose opinions they have sounded in vain, that they DARE not make such a detestable proposal at present. They find that all the sugar-plumbs they can offer to either the Catholics or the Protestants are insufficient to make them swallow a poison that will be deadly to Ireland.

They therefore deny the intent, and insidiously lye by, in hopes of taking the nation by surprise. But, degenerate indeed must be that Peer, who would even whisper a word in behalf of an Union; detestedly corrupt and slavish must be that Commoner who would even wish for a transportation of the Irish Parliament into London.

What adequate representation would even the Peerage of Ireland could be made? what adequate representation of the Commons of Ireland could be sent into the *Parliament of the empire*, (as it would be then affectedly called) that could bear any proportion to the long list of English Peerage, and the five hundred and fifty eight commoners? What recompence could be made for the ruin of Dublin—For ruin must be the consequence of losing our parliament? The metropolis would then have only a College; the Four Courts, and the farce of a Castle Court under the shadow of a powerless deputy Viceroy, for its support. Then grass would grow in Dame-street, and the Mall, the rents of houses would fall eighty per cent. a stop would be put to all buildings, trade would be at an end, and the business of commerce would not occupy a single wing of the ostentatious Custom-house.

The friends of that cursed contrivance may appeal to the present flourishing state of Scotland, and attribute it to the *Union*. But the case is different in respect to Ireland—England and Scotland were two kingdoms in the same island, divided from each other by only a river or ridge of mountains: Ireland is a separate island, disjoined by a dangerous tho' narrow sea: Nature by its situation points out, that it should be an independent state, and that both islands may be united under one head: they are still separate bodies, each possessing its own heart, and its own members. No, the two islands can never be united but by a mutual affection, a mutual intercourse of trade, and a mutual interchange of good offices. For that kind of Union the Irish are—ready.

NORTHERN STAR, 20–23 APRIL 1795

This unfortunate man having been convicted by a jury of his country of an offence of so unpardonable a nature as high treason, would most undoubtedly have suffered the sentence which the law pronounces on so henious a crime, had it not been for the sudden and premature manner of his dissolution; upon the true cause of which doubts have arisen, even in the minds of medical men. His melancholy catastrophe, and the crime for which he was found guilty having been so uncommon in this country, (no person having been indicted for it for upwards of a century,) has justly drawn the attention of the community in a very ample degree on this wretched and unfortunate man.

WALKER'S HIBERNIAN MAGAZINE, MAY 1795

THE SAILOR'S FAREWELL

THEOBALD WOLFE TONE

In the *Cincinnatus*, which left this port on Sunday last for America, sailed with his family, THEOBALD WOLFE TONE, ESQ. late Secretary to the Catholics of Ireland, and Author of several tracts, which had the Union of Irishmen, and the independence of Ireland for their object.

NORTHERN STAR, 15-18 JUNE 1795

Tune, *"The Green Cockade."*

Ye lovers of UNION, of ev'ry degree,
No matter what Trade or Religion ye be,
The right-hand of friendship to you I'll extend,
And hope for your pardon if I should offend.

For the Rights of Man let us always be,
And Unite in the cause that will make us Free,
Till oppression and tyranny's banish'd the land,
We'll fight for our country with heart and hand.

I'm slave to no sect, and from bigotry free,
And follow what conscience still dictates to me;
All men are my brethren who're ready to lend
Their aid to the country, and hand to a friend.

For the Rights of Man, &c.

Let the creatures of *kings*, and the dupes of a priest,
Bow down to a *bauble*, or worship a beast—
Shall an impious prelate, a statesman, or prince,
Set marks to our reason, or bounds to our sense?

For the Rights of Man, &c.

'Divide then and conquer'—the maxim of knaves,
Who have practis'd it long on a nation of slaves—
But the bright Star of Reason will soon let them see
That *Hibernians* were made to UNITE AND BE FREE.

For the Rights of Man, &c.

PADDY'S RESOURCE, BELFAST, 1795

August 13, 1795

This day, on the motion of the Attorney General, Laurance O'Connor, Michael Griffin, Denis Kelly, Andrew Higgins, Thomas King, and William Fitzsimmons, were brought to the bar of the Crown Court, and arraigned before Mr. Justice Finucane of

HIGH TREASON

The indictment was for compassing the King's death, and also for adhering to his enemies. The overt-acts charged are the following:

1st Forming a party of Defenders to assist the French if they should invade Ireland.—2nd Meeting for that purpose.—3 Encouraging a soldier of the North Mayo Militia (Barth. Horan,) to join them, by assuring him that the French would soon land, and they (the prisoners) would *back* them.—4 Seducing *Horan* to become a Defender.—5 Meeting to admit persons previously sworn into this party, and admitting *Horan.*

O'Connor declared that he expected to have been tried at Naas, and that he was not prepared now to be tried in Athy.

Mr. Justice Finucane informed all the prisoners, that they were not bound to be ready for their trial now; that before they were called upon to plead to the indictment just read, the law required that they have a copy of it, and the assistance of two Counsel of their own choice, to advise with them as to their plea.

The Judge then observed, that from the short time allowed for the assizes of this county, five days could not be allowed before trial, as the law required; the assizes would be adjourned to the 31st instant, then to be held at Naas, to accommodate the prisoners.

Counsel were then assigned at the request of the prisoners.

Another indictment, also for High Treason, was read against O'Connor and Griffin, for administering an oath *"to be true to the French,"* and entering the name of the person sworn, as enlisted for that purpose.

BELFAST NEWS-LETTER, 17–21 AUGUST 1795

EXTRACT OF A LETTER FROM A GENTLEMAN IN
THE NEIGHBOURHOOD OF ARMAGH

For some days past that part of the county of Armagh, from the Blackwater Foot towards Cockhill, Tallbridge, and Loughgall, has been in a state of insurrection, by a constant engagement with arms, between the Break-of-Day Men, and Defenders—the latter assembling in great bodies from the neighbouring counties, and threatening to destroy all before them, *if they gain the day, and to divide the lands, &c.*

Mr. Verner of Church-hill, a Magistrate, with a party of the North Mayo Militia, marched on Friday last, and surprized a large body of these deluded people, and took four prisoners; and, on Sunday last, hearing that a large body of the Defenders were assembling at the Blackwater Foot, (called Mahery) he mounted four of the privates of the same militia on his carriage horses, and with the assistance of the three gentlemen and himself, all on horseback, they rode in full gallop to prevent the rioters from crossing the ferry at that place into the county of Tyrone, but many had escaped over the river before their arrival, and they kept up a constant fire on Mr. Verner and his party as they approached to the river, but by the steadiness and perserverance of the militia, and the gentlemen, in that very dangerous and hazardous situation, they took five prisoners and two muskets.

As parties of the military are now stationed at Verner's Bridge, Cockhill, and Tallbridge, and the Magistrates of that part of the country are determined to exert themselves against every description of persons who shall disturb the peace of the county, it is hoped quietness and good order will be restored to a populous neighbourhood, always remarkable for their industry and exertions in the linen manufacture.

BELFAST NEWS-LETTER, 21–25 AUGUST 1795

PRELUDE TO THE FORMATION OF
THE ORANGE ORDER

A renewal of those vile animosities which have disgraced the middle of the county Armagh for "time out of mind," took place at Grangemore, near Portadown, a few days ago. The combatants under the appellation of Peep o' Day Boys and Defenders, continued in a state of hostility on opposite hills, from Thursday last until Monday when a general engagement took place, which terminated in a drawn battle, after seventeen unfortunate wretches lost their lives. We again repeat it, that the Magistrates and other principal inhabitants of that neighbourhood, are extremely criminal in not stepping forward and reconciling these misled wretches. They have no *cause*, whatever, of quarrel, and surely a reconciliation could not be difficult. This business has been erroneously called a *religious* quarrel—the fact is, neither of the parties are of any religion.

NORTHERN STAR, 21–24 SEPTEMBER 1795

TONE ARRIVES IN FRANCE

February, 1796

F *ebruary* 2. I landed at Havre de Grace yesterday, after a rough winter passage from New York of thirty-one days. The town ugly and dirty, with several good houses in alleys, where it is impossible to see them. Lodged at the Hotel de Paix, formerly the Hotel of the Intendant, but reduced to its present state by the Revolution . . .

February 15. Went to Monroe's, the Ambassador, and delivered in my passport and letters. Received very politely by Monroe . . . I inquired of

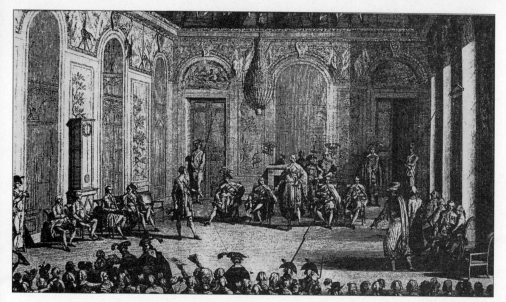

PUBLIC AUDIENCE WITH THE DIRECTORY

him where I was to deliver my despatches. He informed me, at the Minister for Foreign Affairs, and gave me his address . . . I took my leave, and returned to his office for my passport. The Secretary smoked me for an Irishman directly. *A la bonne heure.* Went at three o'clock to the Minister for Foreign Affairs, Rue du Bacq, 471. Delivered my passport, and inquired for someone who spoke English. Introduced immediately to the Chef de Bureau, Lamare, a man of an exceedingly plain appearance. I showed my letter, and told him I wished for an opportunity to deliver it into the Minister's hands . . . He then brought me into a magnificent anti-chamber, where a general officer and another person were writing, and, after a few minutes delay, I was introduced to the Minister, Charles de la Croix, and delivered my letter, which he opened, and seeing it in cypher, he told me, in French, he was much obliged to me for the trouble I had taken, and that the Secretary would give me a receipt, acknowledging the delivery . . .

The Secretary has given me a receipt, of which the following is a translation: "I have received from Mr. James Smith, a letter addressed to the Committee of Public Safety, and which he tells me comes from the citizen Adet, Minister Plenipotentiary of the French Republic at Philadelphia, Paris, 26th Pluviose, third year of the French Republic. The Secretary General of Foreign Affairs, Lamare." I have thus broken the ice. In a day to two I shall return for my passport . . .

February 17. Went at one o'clock to the Minister's bureau, for my passport . . . The principal Secretary . . . told me the Minister wished to see me, and had sent to the Ambassador to learn my *address*. I answered I should attend him whenever he pleased; he replied, "instantly" and, accordingly, I followed him into the Minister's cabinet, who received me very politely. He told me, in French, that he had had the letter I brought decyphered, and laid instantly before the Directoire Executif, who considered the contents as of the greatest importance; that their intentions were, that I should go immediately to a gentleman, whom he would give me a letter to, and, as he spoke both languages perfectly and was confidential, that I should explain myself to him without reserve; that his name was Madgett. I answered, that I knew him by reputation, and had a letter of introduction to him, but did not consider myself at liberty to make myself known to any person, without his approbation. He answered that I might communicate with Madgett, without the least reserve ... I then took my leave, the Minister seeing me to the door ...

I have been at the bureau twice, and both times have been admitted to the Minister's cabinet without a minute's delay. Surely all this looks well ... Set off for Madgett's and delivered my letter. Madgett delighted to see me, tells me he has the greatest expectation our business will be taken up in the most serious manner; that the attention of the French Government is now turned to Ireland, and that the stability and form it had assumed, gave him the strongest hopes of success; that he had written to Hamilton Rowan, about a month since, to request I might come over instantly, in order to confer with the French Government, and determine on the necessary arrangements, and that he had done this by order of the French Executive.

Madgett ... then added, that we should have ten sail of the line, any quantity of arms that were wanted, and such money as was indispensable, but that this last was to be used discreetly, as the demands for it on all quarters were so numerous and urgent; and, that he thought a beginning might be made through America, so as to serve both Ireland and France. That is to say, that military stores might be sent through this channel from France to Ireland, purchased there by proper persons, and provisions, leather, &c. returned in neutral bottoms. I answered, this last measure was impracticable, on account of the vigilance of the Irish Government, and the operation of the gunpowder act, which I explained to him; I then gave him a very short sketch of what I considered the state of Ireland, laying it down as a *positum* that nothing effectual could be done there unless by a landing; that a French army was indispensably necessary as a *point de ralliement*, and I explained to him the

N.B. I shall, in all my negotiations here, press upon them the necessity of a landing being effectuated. If it is not, the people will never move, but to the destruction of a few wretches, and we have had already but too much of that in Ireland . . .

February 18. Breakfast at Madgett's. Long account, on my part, of the state of Ireland when I left it, which will be found substantially in such memoirs as I may prepare. Madgett assures me again that the Government here have their attention turned most seriously to Irish affairs; that they feel that unless they can separate Ireland from England, the latter is invulnerable . . .

February 22. Finished my memorial, and delivered a fair copy, signed, to Madgett for the Minister of Foreign Relations. Madgett in the horrors. He tells me he has had a discourse yesterday for two hours with the Minister, and that the succours he expected will fall very short of what he thought. That the marine of France is in such a state that Government will not hazard a large fleet; and, consequently, that we must be content to steal a march. That they will give 2,000 of their best troops, and arms for 20,000; that they cannot spare Pichegru nor Jourdan; that they will give any quantity of artillery; and, I think he added, what money might be necessary. He also said they would first send proper persons among the Irish prisoners of war, to sound them, and exchange them on the first opportunity. To all this, at which I am not disappointed, I answered, that as to 2,000 men, they might as well send 20. That with regard to myself, I would go if they would send but a corporal's guard, but that my opinion was, that 5,000 was as little as could be landed with any prospect of success . . . He interrupted me to ask who was known in Ireland after Pichegru and Jourdan. I answered, Hoche, especially since his affair at Quiberon. He said he was sure we might have Hoche . . .

February 24. Went at 12 o'clock, in a fright, to the Luxembourg; conning speeches in execrable French, all the way: What shall I say to Carnot? Well, *"whatsoever the Lord putteth in my mouth, that surely shall I utter."* Plucked up a spirit as I drew near the Palace, and mounted the stairs like a lion—Went into the first Bureau that I found open, and demanded at once to see Carnot. The clerks stared a little, but I repeated my demand with a courage truly heroic; on which they instantly submitted, and sent a person to conduct me . . . The folding doors were now thrown open, a bell being previously rung to give notice to the people, that all who had business might present themselves, and citizen Carnot appeared, in the *petit costume of* white satin with crimson robe, richly embroidered . . . I began the discourse by saying, in horrible French, that I had been informed he spoke English. A little, Sir, but I perceive you speak French, and if you please, we will converse in that language . . . I then told him I was an Irishman; that I had been Secretary and Agent to the Catholics of that country, who were about 3,000,000 of people; that I was also in perfect possession of the sentiments of the Dissenters, who were at least 900,000, and that I wished to communicate with him on the actual state of Ireland . . . I proceeded to state, that the sentiments of all those people were unanimous, in favor of France, and eager to throw off the yoke of England . . . I then told him that I came to France by direction and concurrence of the men, who (and here I was at a loss for French word, with which, seeing my embarrassment, he supplied me,) *guided* the two great parties I had mentioned . . . That about the end of November last, I received letters from my friends in Ireland, repeating their instructions in the strongest manner, that I should if possible, force my way to France, and lay the situation of Ireland before its Government . . . That I had the highest respect for the Minister, and that as to Madgett, I had no reason whatsoever to doubt him, but, nevertheless, must be permitted to say, that in my mind, it was a business of too great importance to be transacted with a mere *Commis* . . . I then told Carnot, that, as to my situation, credit, and the station I had filled in Ireland, I begged leave to refer him to James Monroe, the American Ambassador. He seemed struck with this, and then for the first time asked my name. I told him in fact I had two names, my real one and that under which I travelled and was described in my passport. I then took a slip of paper, and wrote the name "James Smith, citoyen Americain," and under it, Theobald Wolfe Tone, which I handed him, adding that my real name was the undermost . . .

Here is a full and true account of my first audience of the Executive Directory of France, in the person of citizen Carnot, the organizer of victory.

JOURNALS OF THEOBALD WOLFE TONE, FEBRUARY 1796

March 10, 1796

I t is stated that in consequence of the arrest of a leading Defender, on
Saturday last, Government has received information of importance,
relative to the principal instigators in the late conspiracy.

BELFAST NEWS-LETTER, 11–14 MARCH 1796

TO THE
PEOPLE OF IRELAND

T here is one point in which persons of every description agree.
The supporter of the government, the democrat and the
moderate man, equally acknowledge, that the present situation
of this country is pregnant with danger.

In the *first* and *second* of these denominations of party, there possibly
may be men, who . . . forget or disregard the incalculable evils that may
be inflicted on their country, by a *violent* pursuit of their respective
measures. The one may suppose, as a quelled insurrection tends to
strengthen the hands of a governing party, that the best method to secure
or increase the power of your present rulers, is to reject every species of
concession, and to provoke a *partial* commotion. The other equally
rejecting every idea, however patriotic, that militates in the smallest
degree against the *entire* completion of his views, relying upon the co-
operation of his associates, and the superior strength of his party, may
also ardently wish to behold the people committed, and oppose any conciliatory measure that would be likely to obstruct the real object of his
pursuit . . .

The democratic party is distinguished for animosity to the measures
of government, the multitude of its adherents, and the zeal which they
display in the propagation of their principles.

They are completely united in dislike to the present system of affairs,
and perhaps nearly as much so in the mode of accomplishing a change,
but with ultimate views the most remote from each other. In a mass
necessarily composed of such heterogeneous materials, there may be
persons so wickedly inclined as to pant for an opportunity of plundering

their neighbours, and *sufficiently ignorant* to expect that a change of government would lead to the fulfillment of their *impracticable* designs. But little are they acquainted with the dispositions of the *people at large*, who allow themselves to be deluded into a belief, that anarchy and plunder of the wealthy are the objects of *their* pursuit. And little do they study the welfare of society, or the *interest of men of property*, who disseminate an accusation so devoid of truth, and so likely (by irritating the minds of the accused) to widen the breach of animosity between them and their accusers.

It cannot be denied by any man who reasons fairly on the subject, that a government thus reformed would at least have *more supporters* and *fewer enemies*, consequently that it would stand on a much firmer foundation, and have more powerful means to defend the country that it could otherwise possess.

At a period like the present, certainly this is no inconsiderable object to be obtained, by those who are interested in the preservation of tranquillity; and, therefore, it is become a sacred duty, that all well-meaning men owe to their country, their families, and themselves, to stand forward *without delay*, and to petition the legislature for a reform.

If men in *middle life* will arouse from their lethargy, and *instantly* exert themselves to procure meetings in the different *counties* where they reside, to address Parliament on the subject before it is *too late*, there is no doubt that the most happy consequences will ensue. All ranks and descriptions will rally around the standard of reform; the most violent among the people; the most enthusiastic admirers of republican doctrines, would, with joy and gladness, embrace a measure productive of so much good to the country, and so great an extension of liberty to themselves.

A LETTER ON THE STATE OF PARTIES AND ON THE SUBJECT OF REFORM,

ADDRESSED TO THE PEOPLE, BELFAST, 1796

THE UNION OF IRISHMEN

For several days past reports were industriously circulated, that those miscreants the Orange-Men, meditated an attack on the town of Belfast, and were determined to destroy the persons and habitations of those in this country who had promoted the UNION OF IRISHMEN—in short, of those who preached the divine doctrine of *"Peace on earth and good will to all men."* Accounts from the county of Armagh had so far corroborated these reports, that on Thursday night last General Nugent, with that attention to the duties of his high station, which has distinguished this officer, thought it necessary to put the garrison of this town in a state of readiness, and to double the guards. The utmost vigilance has been ever since used, and on Saturday last a meeting of a number of those who had borne arms in the Volunteer ranks in this town, was held, when a deputation was appointed to wait on the Sovereign, requesting him to inform General Nugent that they were willing to co-operate with the military under his command, in defence of the town and neighbourhood, in case of necessity.

NORTHERN STAR, 24–28 MARCH 1796

ORANGEMEN CAPITALLY CONVICTED

Henry Winter, James Smith, and Patrick M'Kiernan (Orange-men), were capitally convicted for attacking the dwelling house of George Bell, and firing several shots into it, and received sentence to be executed on Monday the 25th of April instant.

James Moan was tried and convicted for raising Forces to fight a battle against the Orange Men in the County of Armagh, and for recruitment for the Defenders.

THE SUN, 18 APRIL 1796

TO THE
UNITED IRISHMEN

Without any pretentions to a knowledge of the cause of your association, the principles by which you are governed, or the object to which they lead, I take the liberty of addressing to you a few observations, dictated by a sincere regard to the interests of my native land. To investigate the motives that govern the human mind is a work the most arduous and intricate that has ever been undertaken by man. Hence the deceptions and delusions to which we are subject, and hence those disappointments which so often oppose our happiness. I shall therefore proceed with caution and decide with diffidence. In the title of your association I perceive a wish to embrace objects, the extent and importance of which I shall not attempt to divine. — The singular reserve which you think proper to maintain, puts that out of my power. 'Tis this mysterious reserve, your vehement attachment to each other, and the invariable decorum of your conduct, which deserve notice and animadversion.

Why thus run together in secret and solemn union? Are your principles unfit for the light of day? I anticipate your answer. The human mind, you say, is an active principle and cannot be restrained. The Convention Bill and others of similar import, have closed your mouths, and for ever interdicted you from making PUBLIC COMPLAINT—you are forced to mourn in silence, and confine your sorrows to yourselves. The Gunpowder Bill has unnerved your arms and oppressed your spirits, and you seek only to confine your sorrows to yourselves.

The Volunteers who were put down, the Patriots who were banished, the lofty gibbets and reeking scaffolds, sink you into despair, and you seek only to confine your sorrows to yourselves.

The madness of prejudice, the misfortunes of the Catholics, the schemes of the wicked, and the blood which has flowed, harrows up your souls: You ardently seek for union, embrace your countrymen, and confine your sorrows to yourselves.—Well—be this your answer; but, is its melancholy truth a sufficient justification of its expediency?— Or rather—Is the cause and effect justly proportioned to each other? You say, that it is truth impressed upon you by the Author of Nature, that congenial minds should unite, and, that confidence, affection, and virtuous sentiment, is the foundation of private and public felicity.

That whatever you feel, you have nothing to fear; your ploughs and your looms are not neglected; your firesides are not forsaken; you shun idleness and intemperance; you abhor opposition to the existing law; you respect person and property; you abhor insurrection and injustice; you promote *union*, because you are lovers of peace; and ye seek after *truth*, because you are lovers of righteousness.

In this answer I see nothing to blame, and much to praise; keep it constantly in view, and put to shame your gain-sayers; avoid the insidious snares of designing villains, who would assert, or even insinuate, that property should be equallized, or law dispensed with.

The order of society, like the order of nature, must be preserved if we wish its existence.

If such be your practice and principles, what a glorious sight, could we see the whole Irish nation become one family of *United Irishmen!*

NORTHERN STAR, 27–30 MAY 1796

TONE'S BIRTHDAY

*J*une 20. To-day is my birthday—I am thirty-three years old. At that age Alexander had conquered the world; at that age Wolfe had completed his reputation, and expired in the arms of victory. Well, it is not my fault, if I am not as great a man as Alexander or Wolfe. I have as good dispositions for glory as either of them, but I labor under two small obstacles at least—want of talents and want of opportunities; neither of which, I confess, I can help. *Allons! nous verrons.* If I succeed here, I may make some noise in the world yet; and, what is better, the cause to which I am devoted is so just, that I have not one circumstance to reproach myself with. I will endeavour to keep myself as pure as I can, as to the means; as to the end, it is sacred—the liberty and independence of my country first.

JOURNALS OF THEOBALD WOLFE TONE, 20 JUNE 1796

EARL CAMDEN, LORD LIEUTENANT GENERAL
AND GENERAL GOVERNOR OF IRELAND

A party of two hundred of the Royal Artillery, with six pieces of ordnance, marched early on Wednesday morning from Chapelizod, on the route to the Camp in the neighbourhood of Belfast.

THE SUN, 29 JUNE 1796

PREPARATIONS

July 12. *Battle of Aughrim.* As I was sitting in my cabinet studying my tactics, a person knocked at the door, who, on opening it, proved to be a dragoon of the third regiment. He brought me a note from Clarke, informing me that the person he mentioned was arrived, and desired to see me at one o'clock. I ran off directly to the Luxembourg, and was shewed into Fleury's cabinet, where I remained till three, when the door opened, and a very handsome well made young fellow, in a brown coat and nankeen pantaloons, entered, and said, *"Vous vous etes le citoyen Smith?"* I thought he was a chef de bureau, and replied, *"Oui, citoyen, je m'appelle Smith."* He said, *"Vous appelez, aussi, je crois Wolfe Tone?"* I replied, *"Oui, citoyen, c'est mon veritable nom." "Eh bien,"* replied he, *"je suis le General Hoche."* . . . He then said he presumed I was the author of the memorandums which had been transmitted to him. I said I was. Well, said he, there are one or two points I want to consult you on. He then proceeded to ask me, in case of the landing being effectuated, might he rely on finding provisions, and particularly bread? I said it would be impossible to make any arrangements in Ireland, previous to the landing, because of the *surveillance* of the Government, but if that were once accomplished, there would be no want of provisions; that Ireland abounded in cattle, and, as for bread, I saw by the Gazette that there was not only no deficiency of corn, but that she was able to supply England, in a great degree, during the late alarming scarcity in that country, and I assured him, that if the French were once in Ireland, he might rely that, whoever wanted bread, they should not want it.—He seemed satisfied with this, and proceeded to ask me, might we count upon being able to form a provisory Government, either of the Catholic Committee,

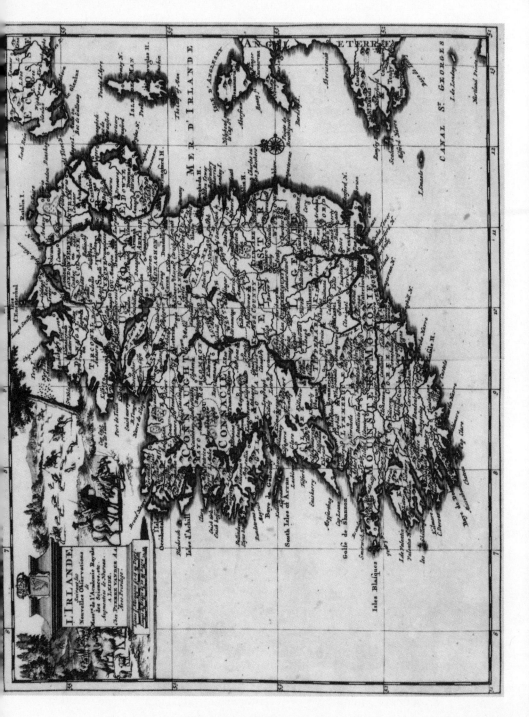

MAP OF IRELAND, PRINTED IN FRANCE

mentioned in my memorials, or of the chiefs of the Defenders? I thought I saw an open here, to come at the number of troops intended for us, and replied, that that would depend on the force which might be landed; if that force were but trifling, I could not pretend to say how they might act, but if it was considerable, I had no doubt of their co-operation. "Undoubtedly," replied he, "men will not sacrifice themselves, when they do not see a reasonable prospect of support; but, if I go, you may be sure I will go in sufficient force." . . .

July 14. *Taking of the Bastile*, 1789. No business! Hoche yesterday praised Sir Sydney Smith, now prisoner in Paris, as a gallant officer: he said, *"Il a une rude reputation en Bretagne,"* and that there was hardly a cape of headland on the coast, which was not marked by some of his exploits. I like to hear one brave man praise another.

July 18. Rose early this morning . . . Called at twelve on Clarke. At last he has got my brevet from the Minister at War. It is for the rank of Chef de Brigade, and bears date the 1st Messidor. (June 19th.) It remains now to be signed by Carnot and Lagarde, which will be done to-day, and to-morrow, at nine, I am to pass muster. . .

July 23. Called at Clarke's, on Fleury; coming out met General Hoche, who desired to see me to-morrow morning, at seven o'clock, in order to talk over our business, and settle about my leaving Paris. That looks like business; Huzza! Huzza!. . .

July 25. Running about all this morning on trade affairs. Damn it! Saw Clarke; he tells me I am to travel with Hoche, and that we set off the 30th, in five days. Huzza!

JOURNALS OF THEOBALD WOLFE TONE, JULY 1796

THE FELONY ACT

Whereas traitorous insurrections have for some time past arisen in various parts of this kingdom, principally promoted and supported by persons associating under the pretended obligation of oaths unlawfully administered: And whereas the penalties for administering and taking such unlawful oaths, enacted by an act passed in the twenty-seventh year of his Majesty's reign, entitled, *An act to prevent tumultuous risings and assemblies, and for the more effectual punishing of persons guilty of outrage, riot, and illegal combination, and of administering and taking unlawful oaths*, have been found insufficient to deter wicked and designing men from administering and taking such oaths: be it enacted by the King's most excellent Majesty, by and with the advice and consent of the lords spiritual and temporal, and commons in this present parliament assembled, and by the authority of the same, That any person or persons who shall administer, or cause to be administered, or be present, aiding and assisting at the administering, or who shall by threats, promises, persuasions, of other undue means, cause, procure, or induce to be taken by any person or persons, upon a book, or otherwise, any oath or engagement, importing to bind the person taking the same, to be of any association, brotherhood, society, or confederacy, formed for seditious purposes, or to disturb the publick peace, or to obey the orders or rules, or commands of any committee, or other body of men, not lawfully constituted, or the commands of any captain, leader, or commander, (not appointed by his Majesty, his heirs and successors) or to assemble at the desire or command of any such captain, leader, commander, or committee, or of any person or persons not having lawful authority, or not to inform or give evidence against any brother, associate, confederate, or other person, or not to reveal or discover his having taken any illegal oath, or done any illegal act, or not to discover any illegal oath or engagement which may be tendered to him, or the import thereof, whether he shall take such oath, or enter into such engagement, or not, being by due course of law convicted thereof, shall be adjudged guilty of felony, and suffer death without benefit of clergy; and every person who shall take such oath or engagement, not being thereto compelled by inevitable necessity, and being by due course of law thereof convicted, shall be adjudged guilty of felony, and be transported for life.

AN ACT MORE EFFECTUALLY TO SUPPRESS INSURRECTIONS, AND PREVENT THE
DISTURBANCE OF THE PUBLICK PEACE, 1796

THE GENERAL IN CHIEF, TO THE EXECUTIVE DIRECTORY

Head-quarters at Etlingen,

23 Messidor, July 11

After the battle of Rastadt, the enemy retreated to the excellent position in front of Etlingen; their right extended towards the Rhine, on the side of Durmersheim, and their left to Rotensolhe, near the Abbey of Frawenalb.

I could not have a doubt but that Prince Charles had already received great reinforcements. Most of the prisoners taken at Rastadt came from the environs of Mentz, and they almost all agreed in saying, that a body of Saxons were expected to arrive that day, with the rest of the divisions of Prince Charles's army, led by Generals Rotze and Venek, and that there was only left on the lower Rhine a body of 30,000 men under General Wartensleben.

I wrote to General St. Cyr to join me immediately by the valley of Murg, with all the troops he could bring with him, without exposing the posts of Fredenstatt and Knubis to danger; I knew these could not arrive till the 8th. I could have wished to attack the enemy sooner, but it was impossible; the repair of the artillery, the fresh supplies of ammunition and horses, and the necessity of reconnoitring the enemy before we attacked them, did not allow us to act before the 9th. I ordered General St. Cyr, who commanded the centre of the army, to turn the enemy's left, and attack all their positions at the source of the river Alb.

General Dessaix, who led the left wing, had orders to attack the corps which the enemy had stationed between the mountains and the Rhine; our left, quite in the rear, was to advance to the village of Etlingen.

General St. Cyr sent General Taponier, with the 21st half brigade of light infantry, and the 31st of the line, with 50 Hussars of the 9th, without artillery, across the mountains, to the Ems, with orders to pass that river, and to push forward to Wibad, in order to turn the enemy's right. Adjutant-general Houel, with the 84th half brigade, and 100 Chasseurs of the 2nd regiment, had orders to attack the post of Frawenalb, and to threaten the left flank of that of Rotensolhe; he reserved for himself the attack of the front of that position, at the head of the 106th half brigade; he had under him Brigadier-generals Lambert and Lecourbe.

This disposition was attended with all the success that could be expected. The enemy made the most determined resistance at Herenald,

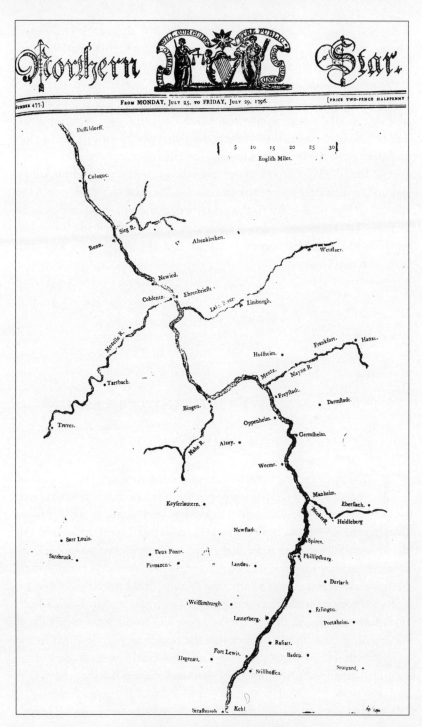

Northern Star.

Number 477.]   From MONDAY, July 25, to FRIDAY, July 29, 1796.   [Price Two-Pence Halfpenny

MAP OF EUROPE, *NORTHERN STAR*, JULY 1796

Frawenalb, and on the heights of Rotensolhe, which were defended by a chosen body of foot; a numerous train of artillery, three battalions of grenadiers, four regiments of infantry, one battalion of Croats, one of light infantry, and four squadrons of horse, had received orders to defend these posts to the last extremity. Our troops displayed an admirable degree of courage and perseverance. Four times we were repulsed, and driven back to the foot of the mountain, which is one of the highest and steepest of the black mountains. The fifth charge, strengthened by a part of the reserve, formed, as nearly as the ground would admit, into a column, completely succeeded; the enemy, pursued on all sides with the bayonet, were totally put to the route; we took from them one piece of cannon, 1100 prisoners, 12 officers, and one of superior rank. Their loss in killed and wounded is enormous; the field of battle was strewed with arms and dead bodies.

NORTHERN STAR, 25–29 JULY 1796

EQUALITY, FRATERNITY AND OPPRESSION

DE LATOCNAYE

The party spirit, political or religious, has weakened very much of late, and I would dare to hope that in ten years it will have ceased to exist. The Catholic religion has very many more followers than has the dominant, which is indeed only the religion of the rich. All the lower classes all over Ireland, the north excepted, are Catholics. They observe Lent and the fast days with a regularity perfectly horrible to a man who wishes only to fast after the manner of the Scotch . . .

I was received with much kindness in this town by Mr. Richardson, with whom I passed three or four days. The country women-folk at Coleraine are, on Sundays, very like the Scotch peasant women in the neighbourhood of Montrose. They are extremely well dressed, their shoulders usually covered by a red mantle. One can hardly believe that this is Ireland.

I walked one day along the river Bann, which flows out of Lough Neagh, a lake of which I shall speak later. Wishing to inform myself of the state of the country, I stopped Mr. Richardson's servant with the horse, and risked going into a cabin and talking with the family, as I was accustomed to do when moving on foot. I praised the country, and said that it was a cruel thing that any should say that the country people were not ready to defend the Constitution, &c., &c. The good folk were very reserved as long as I remained in the cabin, but as soon as I left, I was followed by a young man who had more confidence in me, and who commenced to retail to me the kind of trifling nonsense on which the people of France fed themselves before the Revolution. I was really surprised to hear all this talk about equality, fraternity, and oppression. After a little I asked him what was the oppression of which he complained. He named taxes on wine and beer, and when I asked him if he ever drank the one or the other, he said it was all the same; it was very hard on those who had to pay, with more nonsense of this kind. He spoke also about the reform of Parliament, and complained much of abuses in elections, preached of tolerance, and indulged in philosophical discourse, such as was heard from our foppish talkers before the Revolution. To tell the truth, I returned from my excursion with a poor opinion of the United Irishman.

A FRENCHMAN'S WALK THROUGH IRELAND, 1796–1797

ARREST OF NEILSON AND RUSSELL

F riday [Sept. 16] 1796, Belfast.—"Since 10 o'clock this morning Belfast has been under military government. A troop of horse is before my door. A guard on Haslett's, which is near us. One at Church Lane, the Long Bridge, and every avenue to the town. Haslett is taken; Neilson and Russell have been walking the streets till about an hour ago, when, the Library being broken open, and search being made for them, they delivered themselves up, with one Osborne, Kennedy, printer at the *Star* office, one Shannon, young Teeling, taken, I am told, by Lord Castlereagh, with several more in Lisburn. They are all now at the Library before the Marquis, Castlereagh, Westmeath, Bristow, Banks, etc., and carriages, guards, etc., to take them off to Dublin . . .

Half after 3; the guards are gone from this part of the town. I hope it will not turn out to be what is said, for I think *tampering* with any one base, and with soldiers more than any. It is probable you will soon see these men. 'I was in prison and ye came unto Me.' *You* were there also, and do not let anything prevent your doing a humane and friendly action ... They are taken up for high treason. I hope there will be no irons. Neilson will be easily killed, though he looks bluff. Russell I feel for, as if a younger, rasher brother, though during years of intimacy and confidence I never heard a worse sentiment than his book contained, and to those he has been consistent. I hope you will get seeing them."

LETTER FROM MRS MARTHA McTIER TO DR WILLIAM DRENNAN, 16 SEPTEMBER 1796

ARREST OF WILLIAM ORR

On Monday last Mr. William Orr, near Shane's Castle, and Mr. John Cochran, of Lisburn, were taken up and committed to Carrickfergus gaol: the nature of the charges against them we have not been able to learn.

Yesterday Hugh Morrison, publican in this town, was committed to the County gaol, charge upon oath with endeavouring to induce some of his Majesty's soldiers from their allegiance, and being present when illegal oaths were administered to them, and uttering seditious and treasonable expressions.

BELFAST NEWS-LETTER, 19–23 SEPTEMBER 1796

THE THREATENED INVASION

Oct. 18. The House having resolved itself into a Committee to consider of the paragraph of his majesty's Speech, which relates to the enemy's having manifested an intention of attempting a descent on these kingdoms ...

Mr. *Pitt* rose and said:—After the unanimous vote which the House gave upon the first day of the session, and their general concurrence in that part of the Address which respects a foreign invasion, it would be doing injustice to the feelings which were then expressed, were I to make an apology for calling their attention to the subject on the present occasion. I shall not detain them therefore a single moment in showing the propriety of laying before them at so early a period the measure which I mean this day to propose ... I shall not at present go much at large into the detail of preparations, but merely suggest a general outline of defence, which, if approved of, may be discussed when the bills are afterwards brought in upon the resolutions. The general considerations are few and obvious. The natural defence of this kingdom, in case of invasion, is certainly its naval force. This presents a formidable barrier, in whatever point the enemy may direct their attack. In this department, however, little now remains to be done; our fleet at this moment being more formidable than at any other period of our history. But strong and powerful as it at present is, it is capable of considerable increase, could an additional supply of seamen, or even landsmen, who in a very short time might be

GENERAL LAZARE HOCHE

trained to an adequate knowledge of the naval service, be procured. For this purpose I would suggest a levy upon the different parishes throughout the kingdom ... The committee, however, must be sensible, when a plan of invasion is in agitation—a scheme, which almost at another time would not have been conceived, and an attempt, which, by any other enemy than that with whom we have now to contend, might have been justly deemed impracticable—that a more extensive plan of prevention and of defence is necessary.— In digesting this plan there are two considerations of which we ought not to lose sight. The first is the means (which must not be altogether new) of calling together a land force sufficiently strong to frustrate the attempt, keeping our naval force entirely out of view; and secondly, to adopt such measures in raising this force as shall not materially interfere with the industry, the agriculture, and the commerce of the country. It will be for the House to decide upon the degree to which the former consideration ought to be permitted to interfere with the latter. A primary object will be to raise, and gradually to train, such a force as may in a short time be fit for service. Of all the modes of attaining this object, there is none so expeditious, so effectual, and attended with so little expense, as that of raising a supplementary levy of militia, to be grafted upon the present establishment.

HANSARD'S PARLIAMENTARY DEBATES, 18 OCTOBER 1796

END OF THE FIFTH INVASION — OR — THE DESTRUCTION OF THE FRENCH ARMADA

McCRACKEN AND KEENAN COMMITTED ON A CHARGE OF HIGH TREASON

Sunday night, two persons, charged with High Treason, were brought up to this city from the North, in custody of a Magistrate, and escorted by a squadron of horse. One of their names is McCracken, who was lodged in the county gaol— the other Keenan, who was sent to the New Prison. They were next day brought before Judge BOYD, who committed them on a charge of High Treason.

THE TIMES, 20 OCTOBER 1796

Paris, Sunday, Nov. 13, 1796

MY LORD,—I have reason to believe from the accounts I have received that there are at Brest eleven sail of the line ready, to a certain extent, for sea, and from fifteen to twenty thousand men. The troops are chiefly at Morlaix, and it is supposed that an expedition is meditated against Ireland. In order to encourage the soldiers to embark, the most exaggerated reports are spread of the temper of that country, and of the successful insurrections which have taken place in it. The idea of a descent on the coast of England from Dunkirk, Ostend and Flushing seems no longer to be a prevalent one, and I understand the embargo is taken off.

I have, &c.,

MALMESBURY

DIARIES AND CORRESPONDENCE OF JAMES HARRIS, 1ST EARL OF MALMESBURY, 1796

THE ATTEMPTED INVASION OF IRELAND

December 1, 2. Received my order to embark on board the *Indomptable* of 80 guns, Capt. Bedout. Packed up directly, and wrote a long letter of directions to my wife, in which I detailed every thing I thought necessary, and advised her, in case of anything happening to me, to return to America, and settle in Georgia or Carolina. I enclosed this under cover to Madgett, and, at two o'clock, arrived on board. We have a most magnificent vessel. To-day I command the troops, as the highest in rank, but to-morrow I shall be superseded, I expect, by the arrival of the whole Etat Major. I hope in God we are about to set out at last. I see, by a proclamation of the Lord Lieutenant, that the north of Ireland is in a flame; if we arrive safe, we shall not do much to extinguish it. Well, we shall see . . .

December 12. The Etat Major came aboard last night; we are seven in the great cabin, including a lady in boy's clothes, the wife of a Commissaire, one Ragoneau. By what I see we have a little army of Commissaries, who are going to Ireland to make their fortunes. If we arrive safe, I think I will keep my eye a little upon these gentlemen.

December 15. At 11 o'clock this morning the signal was made to heave short, and I believe we are now going to sail in downright earnest. There is a signal also at the point for four sail of enemies in the offing; it is most delicious weather, and the sun is as warm and as bright as in the month of May . . . We are all in high spirits, and the troops are as gay as if they were going to a ball. With our 15,000, or more correctly, 13,975 men, I would not have the least doubt of our beating 30,000 of such as will be opposed to us; that is to say, if we reach our destination. The signal is now flying to get under way, so one way or other, the affair will be at last brought to a decision, and God knows how sincerely I rejoice at it. The wind is right aft, Huzza! . . .

December 19. This morning, at eight, signal of a fleet in the offing; Branlebas General; rose directly and made my toilet, so now I am ready, *ou pour les Anglais, ou pour les Anglaises.* I see about a dozen sail, but whether they are friends or enemies God knows. It is a stark calm, so that we do not move an inch even with our studding sails; but here we lie rolling like so many logs on the water. It is most inconceivably provoking; two frigates that were ordered to reconnoitre, have not advanced one hundred yards in an hour, with all the canvass out; it is now nine o'clock; damn it to hell for a calm, and in the middle of December. Well, it cannot last long . . .

The wind, which favored us thus far, is chopped about, and is now right in our teeth; that is provoking enough. If we had a fair wind we should be in Bantry Bay to-morrow morning. At half-past one, hailed by a lugger, which informed us of the loss of the *Seduisant,* a seventy-four of our squadron, the first night of our departure, with five hundred and fifty men of the ninety-fourth Demi-brigade, of whom she saved thirty-three. It happened near the same spot where we were in such imminent danger. I was mistaken above in saying that the *Fraternité* was with the squadron which joined us; it is Admiral Nielly's frigate, and we know nothing of the other, which has thrown us all into the greatest anxiety . . .

December 20. Last night, in moderate weather, we contrived to separate again, and this morning, at eight o'clock, we are but fifteen sail in company, with a foul wind, and hazy. I am in horrible ill humor, and it is no wonder. We shall lie beating about here, within thirty leagues of Cape Clear, until the English come and catch us, which will be truly agreeable . . .

December 21. Last night, just at sunset, signal for seven sail in the offing; all in high spirits, in hopes that it is our comrades . . . We are thirty-five sail in company, and seven or eight absent. Is that such a separation of our force, as, under all the circumstances, will warrant our following the letter of our orders, to the certain failure of the expedition? If Grouchy and Bouvet be men of spirit and decision, they will land immediately, and trust to their success for justification. If they be not, and if this day passes without our seeing the General, I much fear the game is up. I am in undescribable anxiety . . . There cannot be imagined a situation more provokingly tantalizing than mine at this moment, within view, almost within reach of my native land, and uncertain whether I shall ever set my foot on it. We are now, nine o'clock, at the rendezvous appointed; stood in for the coast till twelve, when we were near enough to toss a biscuit ashore; at twelve tacked and stood out again, so now we have begun our cruise of five days in all its forms, and shall, in obedience to the letter of our instructions, ruin the expedition, and destroy the remnant of the French navy, with a precision and punctuality which will be truly edifying. We opened Bantry Bay, and, in all my life, rage never entered so deeply into my heart as when we turned our backs on the coast . . .

December 22. This morning, at eight, we have neared Bantry Bay considerably, but the fleet is terribly scattered; no news of the *Fraternité*; I believe it is the first instance of an Admiral in a clean frigate, with moderate weather, and moonlight nights, parting company with his fleet. Captain Grammont, our first Lieutenant, told me his opinion is that she is either taken or lost, and, in either event, it is a terrible blow to us. All rests now upon Grouchy, and I hope he may turn out well: he has a glorious game in his hands, if he has spirits and talent to play it . . . We are gaining the Bay by slow degrees, with a head wind at east, where it has hung these five weeks. To-night we hope, if nothing extraordinary happens, to cast anchor in the mouth of the Bay, and work up to-morrow morning; these delays are dreadful to my impatience. I am now so near the shore that I can see, distinctly, two old castles, yet I am utterly uncertain whether I shall ever set foot on it . . .

December 23. Last night it blew a heavy gale from the eastward with snow, so that the mountains are covered this morning, which will render our bivouacs extremely amusing . . . The wind is still high, and, as usual, right ahead; and I dread a visit from the English, and altogether I am in great uneasiness. Oh! that we were once ashore, let what might ensue after; I am sick to the very soul of this suspense. It is curious to see how things are managed in this best of all possible worlds. We are here, sixteen sail, great and small, scattered up and down in a noble bay, and so dispersed that there are not two together in any spot, save one, and there they are now so close, that if it blows tonight as it did last night, they will inevitably run foul of each other, unless one of them prefers driving on shore. We lie in this disorder, expecting a visit from the English every hour, without taking a single step for our defence, even to the common one of having a frigate in the harbor's mouth, to give us notice of their approach . . .

Tonight, on examining the returns with Waudré, Chef d'Etat Major of the Artillery, I find our means so reduced by the absence of the missing, that I think it hardly possible to make an attempt here, with any prospect of success; in consequence, I took Cherin into the Captain's room, and told him frankly my opinion of our actual state, and that I thought it our duty, since we must look upon the main object as now unattainable, unless the whole of our friends returned to-morrow, and the English gave us our own time, which was hardly to be expected, to see what could be done for the honor and interest of the Republic, with the force which remained in our hands, and I proposed to him to give me the Legion des Francs, a company of Artillerie legere, and as many officers as desired to come volunteers in the expedition, with what arms and stores remained, which are now reduced, by our separation, to four field pieces, 20,000 firelocks at most, 1,000 lb of powder, and 3,000,000 cartridges, and to land us in Sligo Bay, and let us make the best of our way; if we succeeded, the Republic would gain infinitely in reputation and interest, and, if we failed, the loss would be trifling, as the expense was already incurred, and as for the legion, he knew what kind of desperadoes it was composed of, and for what purpose; consequently, in the worst event, the Republic would be well rid of them; finally, I added that though I asked the command, it was on the supposition that none of the Generals would risque their reputations on such a desperate enterprise, and that if another was found, I would be content to go as a simple volunteer . . .

The discourse rested there, and to-morrow we shall see more, if we are not agreeably surprised, early in the morning, by a visit from the English, which is highly probable. I am now so near the shore, that I can in a manner touch the sides of Bantry Bay with my right and left hand, yet God knows whether I shall ever tread again on Irish ground . . .

December 24. This morning the whole Etat Major has been miraculously converted, and it was agreed, in full council, that General Cherin, Colonel Waudré, Chef d'Etat Major of the Artillery, and myself, should go aboard the *Immortalité* and press General Grouchy in the strongest manner, to proceed on the expedition, with the ruins of our scattered army. Accordingly, we made a signal to speak with the Admiral, and in about an hour we were aboard. I must do Grouchy justice to say, that the moment we gave our opinion in favor of proceeding, he took his part decidedly, and like a man of spirit; he instantly set about preparing the *ordre de bataille*, and we finished it without delay ... I never saw the French character better exemplified, than in this morning's business. Well, at last I believe we are about to disembark ... I learn from a pilot whom I found aboard the *Admiral*, that my friend Hutchins lives within two miles of Bantry, and is now at home, so perhaps I may see him to-morrow; I wonder what kind of meeting we shall have ...

December 25. These memorandums are a strange mixture. Sometimes I am in preposterously high spirits, and at other times I am as dejected, according to the posture of our affairs. Last night I had the strongest expectations that to-day we should debark, but at two this morning I was awakened by the wind. I rose immediately, and wrapping myself in my great coat, walked for an hour in the gallery, devoured by the most gloomy reflections. The wind continues right ahead, so that it is absolutely impossible to work up to the landing place, and God knows when it will change ...

December 26. Last night, at half after six o'clock, in a heavy gale of wind still from the east, we were surprised by the Admiral's frigate running under our quarter, and hailing the *Indomptable*, with orders to cut our cable and put to sea instantly; the frigate then pursued her course, leaving us all in the utmost astonishment. Our first idea was that it might be an English frigate, lurking in the bottom of the bay, which took advantage of the storm and darkness of the night to make her escape, and wished to separate our squadron by this stratagem; for it seems utterly incredible, that an Admiral should cut and run in this manner, without any previous signal of any kind to warn the fleet, and that the first notice we should have of his intention, should be his hailing us in this extraordinary manner, with such unexpected and peremptory orders. After a short consultation with his officers, (considering the storm, the darkness of the night, that we have two anchors out and only one spare one in the hold,) Captain Bedout resolved to wait, at all events, till to-morrow morning, in order to ascertain whether it was really the Admiral who hailed us. The morning is now come, the gale continues, and the fog is so thick that we cannot see a ship's length ahead; so here we lie in the utmost uncertainty and anxiety. In all probability we are now left without Admiral or General; if so, Cherin will command the troops, and Bedout the fleet, but, at all events, there is an end of the expedition.

December 28. Last night it blew a perfect hurricane. At one this morning, a dreadful sea took the ship in the quarter, stove in the quarter gallery, and one of the dead-lights in the great cabin, which was instantly filled with water to the depth of three feet. The cots of the officers were almost torn down, and themselves and their trunks floated about the cabin. For my part, I had just fallen asleep when wakened by the shock, of which I first did not comprehend the meaning; but hearing the water distinctly rolling in the cabin beneath me, and two or three of the officers mounting in their shirts, as wet as if they had risen from the bottom of the sea, I can safely say that I had perfect command of myself during the few terrible minutes which I passed in this situation, and I was not, I believe, more afraid than any of those about me. I resigned myself to my fate, which I verily thought was inevitable, and I could have died like a man. Immediately after this blow, the wind abated, and, at daylight, having run nine knots an hour under one jib only, during the hurricane, we found ourselves at the rendezvous, having parted company with three ships of the line and the frigate, which makes our *sixth* separation. The frigate *Coquille* joined us in the course of the day, which we spent standing off and on the shore, without being joined by any of our missing companions.

December 29. At four this morning, the Commodore made the signal to steer for France: so, there is an end to our expedition for the present;

perhaps for ever. I spent all yesterday in my hammock, partly through sea-sickness, and much more through vexation. At ten, we made prize of an unfortunate brig, bound from Lisbon to Cork, laden with salt, which we sunk.

December 30, 31. On our way to Brest. It will be well supposed I am in no great humor to make memorandums. This is the last day of the year 1796, which has been a very remarkable one in my history.

JOURNALS OF THEOBALD WOLFE TONE,

DECEMBER 1796

LIEUTENANT G. PROSHEAU

Lord Bridport with his fleet, has been off the Irish coast since Sunday last: He came directly for it from England, as soon as the wind would permit . . .

We hear that above 30,000 musquets have been given out by order of Government, to the various volunteer corps of infantry in this kingdom; and more are wanting. The volunteer cavalry in the country is at least double the number of the former—the whole must therefore make a force at present of 90,000, exclusive of the regular army and militia.

Sufficient praise cannot be given to the inhabitants of the City and County of Cork, for their patriotic zeal on the recent perilous occasion. The Cork Legion of Volunteers, under the command of Lord DONOUGHMORE, and officered in all the subaltern departments by Catholics and Protestants indiscriminately, manifested the utmost alacrity for the public service; and the whole of the farmers and peasantry in that respectable county, who are mostly Catholics, seemed actuated by one soul, and united in one zeal, to aid in the defence of their country.

THE TIMES, 20 JANUARY 1797

NORTHERN STAR

In consequence of the STAR OFFICE being taken possession of this Morning, by Colonel Barber, a King's Messenger, and Military Guard, the Proprietors of the Newspaper have it not in their power to Publish this day: for this disappointment of their numerous Friends and Readers they are sincerely sorry; and so soon as this *restraint of Government* permits them to resume the regular Publication of the Paper, the Public may rely upon being regularly supplied with it, on the accustomed Plan.

Colonel Barber, the Sovereign, and a Military Guard visited Mr. O'Connor's house early this Morning; upon enquiry they found he was not at home, they then searched for and carried off some Papers, and upon their return to town, arrested Robert and William Simms, the only Proprietors of the Paper now out of Jail—so that independent of the Seizure and Occupation of the Printing Office, by the Officers of Government, the Arrest of these Gentlemen might be a sufficient Apology for the want of publication this Day.

Our Friends who owe us Advertisements and Newspaper Accounts, will please, in the mean time, pay them to MATHEW SMITH, Bridge Street.

BELFAST, 3 FEBRUARY 1797

UNWELCOME NEWS

February 19, 20, 21, 22. I see by the Courier of the 14th instant, that Robert and William Simms are arrested for publishing Arthur O'Connor's letter, as it should seem, for the account is rather confused. I collect from another paragraph in the same paper, that they were released on the 9th; but O'Connor remains in custody ...

There is now scarcely one of my friends in Ireland but is in prison, and most of them in peril of their lives; for the system of terror is carried as far there, as ever it was in France in the time of Robespierre.

JOURNALS OF THEOBALD WOLFE TONE, FEBRUARY 1797

A most horrid murder was committed near Dromore, on the lands of Gillhall, on Monday morning last, upon a poor man of the name of Macdowell. He was known to be an Orange Man, and had improvidently dropt some hints that he could make great discoveries against the United Irishmen; the next night, a number of those desperate wretches, amounting to thirty, surrounded the house, forced the door and windows, dragged him from his bed into the highway, shot several balls through his head and body, and stabbed him with their bayonets in an hundred places. No sooner had the account reached Dromore, than the Yeomen marched out under Captain Brush, searched the neighbourhood, and seized one of the murderers—his name, Flack: he was positively sworn to by the unhappy wife and her daughter, and the Coroner's Inquest gave their verdict—that Macdowell's death was occasioned by various wounds given by several people, one of whom was Flack.

A very liberal Subscription was immediately raised for the poor woman and her children, and they were brought into Dromore for their protection.

THE SUN, 15 APRIL 1797

UNITED IRISHMEN IMPRISONED IN KILMAINHAM

Saturday, the following persons, charged with being United Irishmen, were brought into town from the North, under an escort of two troops of cavalry. They were taken to the Castle of Dublin, from which they were committed to the prison of Kilmainham;

Rev. Sinclair Kilburne, Dissenting Clergyman, Dr. Crawford, of Lisburn, Hugh Kirkwood, William Templeton, James Burnside, William Keane, James Haffey, Daniel Toland, Jacob Nicholson, Thomas Jackson, Henry Spear, Robert Neilson, Alexander Clarke, John Harrison, James Grier, John Kennedy, Wm. McCracken, William McManus, John Barret.

THE TIMES, 1 MAY 1797

KILMAINHAM BARRACKS, DUBLIN

FURTHER REPORT FROM
THE COMMITTEE OF SECRECY

REPORTED BY THE RIGHT
HONOURABLE MR. SECRETARY PELHAM

MR. SPEAKER,

THE Committee of Secrecy, appointed to take into Consideration the Papers presented to the House on the twenty ninth Day of April last by the Right Honourable Mr. Secretary Pelham, have directed me to report as follows:

YOUR Committee having taken into their Consideration the Papers referred to them, have thought it consistent with their Dury to carry their Enquiries back to the Period of Commencement of the Societies styling themselves *United Irishmen*.

It appears that soon after the French Revolution certain Individuals, encouraged by the Example of France, aimed at the Overthrow of the existing Laws and Constitution of this Kingdom, and the Establishment of a Republic unconnected with Great Britain: that they have been encouraged to proceed to this Attempt by an Expectation of Aid from France, and the Co-operation of certain disaffected and seditous Societies in Great Britain entertaining similar Views.

It appears to your Committee that their Hopes of Success in this apparently improbable Design are derived from their Expectations of being able to infuse into the Minds of the lower Orders of the People an Idea that they are in a State of Oppression and Misery: that the King, the Houses of Lords and Commons, with the Magistracy, Clergy and Gentry of the Country, are the Cause of their Oppression: that the Society of United Irishmen are their sole Protectors and Defenders; and that the Connexion between Great Britain and Ireland is inconsistent with the Happiness and Independence of this Kingdom.

It appears to your Committee that to effect their Purposes they have organized with great Address and supported with equal Activity a System plausible in its Name, and which by a Combination of certain specious Propositions with Principles destructive of the Laws and Constitution of this Kingdom, leads in a Manner the most insidious to Anarchy, Confiscation of Property, and the Extermination of its Proprietors.

It appears to your Committee that in the original Formation of this Society, its Authors, to avoid alarming the Feelings of those who were not prepared at once to go the full Extent of their dangerous and traitorous Designs, held forth Catholic Emancipation and Parliamentary Reform as the ostensible Objects of their Union: but their real Purposes were to separate Great Britain

THOMAS REYNOLDS

from Ireland and to subvert the present Constitution, as will appear more fully from the following Explanation given by Mr. Theobald Wolfe Tone, one of the original Framers of the Institution, in a Letter addressed to his Friends at Belfast, and containing Resolutions and Declarations upon which the Institution was formed:

"The foregoing contain my true and sincere Opinion of the State of this Country, so far as in the present Juncture it may be advisable to publish it. They certainly fall short of the Truth, but Truth itself must sometimes condescend to temporize; my unalterable Opinion is that the Bane of Irish Prosperity is in the Influence of England; I believe that Influence will ever be extended while the

Connection between the two Countries continues; nevertheless, as I know that Opinion is for the present too hardy, though a very little Time may establish it universally, I have not made it a Part of the Resolutions; I have only proposed to set up a reformed Parliament as a Barrier against that Mischief which every honest Man that will open his Eyes must see in every Instance overbears the Interest of Ireland: I have not said one Word that looks like a Wish for Separation, though I give it to you and your Friends as my most decided Opinion that such an Event would be a Regeneration to this Country" . . .

Your Committee then directed their Enquiries to the Means by which the Papers referred to them in consequence of the Lord Lieutenant's Message had been procured; and in order the better to ascertain the Credit to be given to their Contents they examined the Persons by whom they have been taken, from whence it appears that upon Information being given of certain Societies or Committees being appointed to assemble at the House of John Alexander in the Town of Belfast at the Hour of eight o'Clock on Friday the 14th of April last, Colonel Barber, with a Detachment of the Army, went to the said House, where two Societies were then actually sitting.

Mr. Fox, Store-keeper of the Ordnance, under the Direction of Colonel Barber entered one of the Rooms in which one of the Committees or Societies was sitting, with their Papers before them, round a Table, and their Secretary in the Chair; and it appears in the Minutebook that the Society had adjourned from the 9th to the 14th of April, the Day on which they were arrested, to sit at the said House.

Lieutenant Ellison of the Artillery entered another Room in the same House where another Committee was sitting; the Papers belonging to that Committee or Society were in the Hat of a Person who sat at the Head of the Table, and appears from the Papers to have been the Secretary of that Society. At the same Time Mr. Atkinson, High Constable of Belfast found concealed in another Room of the same House, Papers purporting to belong to another Committee or Society, viz. the eightieth Society.

These Papers consist of,

1. The printed Declaration and Constitution of the United Irishmen.
2. Minutes of the Proceedings of two of the Societies.

3. Reports from Provincial and County Committees.
4. A Report from the Military Committee.
5. Forms of the Oath of an Officer and of a Soldier.
6. Names of some of the Society, with the Arms that they possess.
7. Size Roll of the Society.
8. A List of the Families that have received Relief.
9. Resolutions of the united Societies of Donaghadee and its Vicinity.
10. Other loose Notes and Papers of their Proceedings.

JOURNALS OF THE HOUSE OF COMMONS, IRELAND, MAY 1797

LETTER FROM LORD CLIFDEN TO LORD COLCHESTER

Dublin, May 15th, 1797

My dear Abbot,—I return you many thanks for yours of the fifth and tenth. This last mutiny at Portsmouth excited lively sensations here. The loyal were dismayed even to make one laugh. The United Irishmen were elated even to make one rage and swear; both parties are now more tranquil. I hope to send you by this night's mail the reports of the secret committees of the Lords and Commons. Such a system of treason has seldom been seen. The North is deeply infected. The Southern districts are yet, I hope, pure. There have been in the course of last week some actions in the North, in one of which fifty yeomen defeated 300 United Men, and cut many to pieces. In a second about 100 Dublin militia, Dundalk yeomanry cavalry, and Watkin's Ancient British Fencibles, defeated about 1000, and cut a vast number to pieces. There were about sixty militia, the rest cavalry. I hope to go to my house at Gouran to take the command of my yeomanry in about a fortnight. I am delayed in town by measures to be brought forward in Parliament in consequence of the reports. Every effort has been made to seduce the militia and army with no effect. There is a vast force now in this country, and more coming from Britain. Many lives must be lost, but these traitors will in the end be exterminated. If the war goes on and the French effect a landing here, which they will certainly attempt, this island will be the scene of blood and confusion for a long time; but in the end Britain, aided by the property of the country, must re-conquer it. I had no conception, till lately, how widely and deeply the roots of insurrection spread. I feel happy that my wife, children, and all I hold most dear, are safe and at a distance from the flame that may consume this land. I think my property will, in the end, be secured to my family; and for the danger, it must be faced, and I think, come what may, though many may fall, the good cause will prevail. Notwithstanding the unpleasant prospect I feel in good spirits, which I reckon a positive good, for many appear in strange and most useless dismay.

I am, dear Sir, yours very sincerely,

CLIFDEN

DIARY OF LORD COLCHESTER, MAY 1797

CORNWALLIS IS SENT TO IRELAND

The report of the day is, that the Marquis Cornwallis, instead of going out to India, is to be sent to Ireland, as Commander in Chief, invested with very great powers; and that Government have at length determined to ameliorate the condition of people as much as possible. Catholic Emancipation is said to be one part of their plan.

BELFAST NEWS-LETTER, 22 MAY 1797

EXECUTION OF FOUR PRIVATES OF THE MONAGHAN MILITIA

On Tuesday last, the 16th, a most awful spectacle took place at the camp at Blaris Warren; four privates of the Monaghan Militia, in pursuance of the sentence of a Court Martial, were shot. These men had been seduced from their allegiance by the United Irishmen; they had engaged to desert from their officers upon a signal; and were actually appointed officers, and had received commissions to act in a rebel corps. The enormity of their offences was of that magnitude, that the lenity of Government could not be extended to them, and the sentence of the law was accordingly executed. The whole of the execution was conducted with the greatest solemnity; the procession of the troops from Belfast was marked by its regularity and silence. On the ground were drawn up a detachment of the 22nd dragoons, a detachment of the Royal artillery, the 64th regiment, the 3rd battalion of light infantry, the Monaghan and Carlow regiments of Militia, the Bredalbane and Argyle fencibles. After the execution, the troops marched in ordinary time by the bodies, which had been conveyed to the church yard and the ceremony closed, leaving the strongest symptoms of impression on all the spectators.

THE TIMES, 23 MAY 1797

THE RESOLUTIONS OF THE
ORANGE SOCIETIES OF ULSTER

At a Meeting of the Masters of the different *Orange Societies* in the Province of ULSTER, held in the City of ARMAGH, on Sunday the 21st of May, 1797, the following Resolutions were unanimously agreed to:

JAMES SLOAN, CHAIRMAN.

We, having seen our Association calumniated and stigmatized, our obligations belied and exaggerated, and ourselves abused and insulted by a coalition of traitors, styling themselves *United Irishmen*; have determined in this public manner to declare the principles upon which our glorious institution is established.

1st, We associate together to defend ourselves and our properties, to preserve the peace of the country, to support our King and Constitution, and to maintain the *Protestant Ascendancy*, for which our ancestors fought and conquered; in short, to uphold the present system and establishment at the risk of our lives, in opposition to the wicked schemes of rebels of all descriptions.

2nd, Our Association, being entirely composed of *Protestants*, has afforded an opportunity to people who undeservedly assume the appellation of *Protestants*, to insinuate to the *Roman Catholics* of IRELAND, that we are sworn to extirpate and destroy them, which infamous charge we thus openly deny and disavow. Our obligation binds us to second and protect the existing laws of the land; and so long as we remain under the influence of that obligation, the loyal, well behaved man, may fear no injury of any sort from us.

3rd, We earnestly request that the several Members of Administration in this country, will not suffer themselves to be prejudiced against us by the unfounded calumnies of unprincipled traitors, of ambitious disposi-tions, and desperate circumstances, who detest us for no other cause than our unshaken loyalty; and who are using every exertion to encrease their consequence, and repair their shattered fortunes, by plunging the kingdom in all the horrors of rebellion, anarchy, and civil war. And we likewise request the nation at large, to believe our most solemn assurance, that there is no body of men more strongly bound to support, or more firmly attached to the Government of the Empire, than the ORANGE MEN OF IRELAND.

4th, We further warmly invite Gentlemen of property to reside in the country, in order that we may enrol ourselves as District Corps under them: And as two Guineas (Government allowance) is not a sufficient sum for clothing a soldier, we entreat Gentlemen to subscribe whatever they may think proper for that necessary purpose; many an honest fellow having no personal property to contend for, nor any other objects than the laudable, patriotic ties of our association.

5th, Resolved, That these our Resolutions shall be published in the *Belfast News-Letter.* Signed by Order

ABRAHAM DAVISON, SECRETARY.

BELFAST NEWS-LETTER, 29 MAY 1797

CAPTURE OF FORGE FOR MAKING PIKES

At four o'clock on the evening of Thursday the 25th inst. Lieutenant General LAKE directed Colonel BARBER and Mr. Fox (Town Major) to proceed with as much expedition as pos-sible, to the Cotton Manufactory of *Robert Armstrong*, on the Falls road, near Belfast. Arriving there before two persons who were on the watch could give an alarm, they caught a smith and his assistant forging pikes. On threatening them with immediate death, they produced sixteen they had secreted in an adjacent house, newly forged. A detachment from the Monaghan Militia, and some Yeomanry who followed, were so much incensed at seeing these implements of destruction, that they levelled the forge to the ground. The pikes were hung round the villains, who were brought prisoners to town. More of these weapons have been since discovered.

Yesterday another blacksmith *James Adams* from Island Magee, was brought in by a Detachment of the Artillery. Some pikes were stuck through his hat, and others hung round him.

On Tuesday *John McClure* was apprehended on a charge of High Treason.

THE SUN, 2 JUNE 1797

A HORRID CONSPIRACY

A horrid revolutionary conspiracy has been discovered at Newry, by searching upon information the house of Mr. Lawson in that town, where was found concealed a number of pikes, a pattern for a rebel uniform, and several papers of revolutionary organization. Struck with remorse at his guilt, this man has acknowledged his atrocity, and discovered his accomplices, some of whom have been apprehended, and others have fled. Among those taken up are, Mr. Gordon, Merchant; Mr. Walker, Merchant; Mr. F. Glenny, Merchant; Mr. Lawson, Bookseller; Mr. Harris, Mr. Melling, &c. and they are sent under a strong guard to Blaris camp.

THE TIMES, 5 JUNE 1797

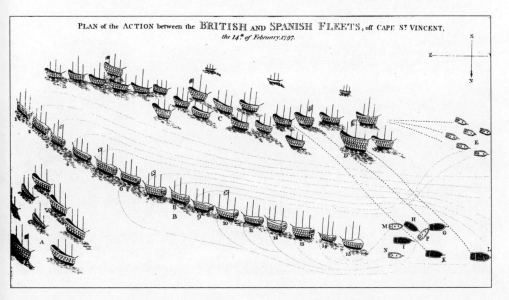

On the 11th inst. the following prisoners were brought into Belfast, and committed to the Artillery Guard-house, charged with seditious practices, John Ballentine, of Rasharken; James M'Anally, from Aughagasen, County of Antrim; and Thomas Thompson, George Templeton, and John Templeton, from Richmond.

THE TIMES, 22 JUNE 1797

ARREST OF UNITED IRISHMEN

The eighteen persons apprehended in the county of Down on Thursday night last, are supposed to have been active leaders, and agitators among the United Irishmen.

BELFAST NEWS-LETTER, 26 JUNE 1796

BELFAST

On the 11th inst. the following prisoners were sent from Randlestown and Shane's Castle, by Lord O'Neill, and committed to the Artillery Guard-room in this town, charged with seditious practices, viz. Dr. Robert Magee, Samuel Orr, James Boreland, Christopher Ryans, Wm. Mulligan, Samuel Walker, Peter Byrnes, Wm. Fallen, Robert Armstrong and John McAlister.

THE TIMES, 26 JULY 1797

TRIAL OF WILLIAM ORR, FOR IMPOSING UNLAWFUL OATHS

Hugh Wheatley, Soldier in the Fife Fencibles, said, that when at Antrim, in April 1796, a person named Campbell introduced him to the Prisoner, and they went to a house where several persons were met. They put a vote, whether he, the witness, should get a copy of the Constitution Book: they all agreed he should and then the Prisoner, who was Chairman, swore him to keep the secrets of United Irishmen, and not to give evidence against any of them. They then gave him the signs of the Society, how they knew each other. These were, 1st, Lift up the right hand, and draw it down over the right side of the face. 2nd, Lift the left hand, and draw it down the left side of the face. 3rd, The two persons were to shake hands by the left hand. 4th, Say: "What do you know?"—"I know U."—"What do you know more?"—"I know T. or any other letter of the words Unity or United."—He was also to swear in as many of the Regiment as he could. When seven were sworn, they were to form a Committee; and then the Book of the Constitution would inform them what to do more. He was also informed by the Prisoner that they were to obtain reform in Parliament; but if it was refused, they would have the military and a number of armed men to effect it.

The Witness was cross-examined by Mr. Curran, but was clear in his evidence.

John Lindsay, another Soldier in the Fife Fencibles, supported the foregoing Witness in almost every particular.

Some Witnesses were produced for the Prisoner, to invalidate the above evidence, but failed. The Jury were inclosed at seven in the evening, and continued so till six in the morning, when they came into Court, and returned a verdict of *Guilty—Death*.

The jury then recommended him to mercy.

It is much to the honour of BARON YELVERTON that we have to observe, that in pronouncing sentence on this unhappy man, he was so deeply affected as scaracely to be able, articulately, to conclude a very impressive address. The tears gushed from his eyes, and, covering his face with both his hands, his Lordship, greatly agitated, remained in that situation several minutes. In this address, the Baron told Mr. Orr, that though recommended to mercy by the Jury, he thought it would be the greatest cruelty to flatter him with any hopes of a remission of the sentence, which had been his painful office to pronounce, and strongly recommended to him to make the best use of his time in making his peace with God, and in preparing for that atonement which he was destined to make to the offended Laws of his Country.

Mr. Orr is a very respectable Farmer, and a man of property, in the neighbourhood of Antrim, where he has resided all his life-time with a fair and unblemished character. He appears to be about 30 or 32 years of age, remarkably good looking, and much the appearance of a Gentleman. He has six children by a very amiable wife, who has been his constant companion in prison, and who is at this moment far advanced in pregnancy. Her distress may be conceived, but it cannot be expressed.

After sentence was pronounced, Mr. Orr requested to be allowed to say a few words.—It was to this effect: Feeling as he did, the strongest conviction of his innocence, which he called upon God to witness, he could not help saying, that the evidences against him were perjured; and with respect to the Jury who had found him guilty, awful as his present situation was, he thought himself comparatively happier than they.

THE SUN, 30 SEPTEMBER 1797

THE DYING DECLARATION OF WILLIAM ORR

The following is the DYING DECLARATION of Mr. Orr as it came to us:

My Friends and Countrymen,

In the thirty-first year of my life, I have been sentenced to die upon the gallows, and this sentence has been in pursuance of a verdict of twelve men, who should have been indifferently and impartially chosen; how far they have been so, I leave to that country from which they have been chosen, to determine; and how far they have discharged their duty, I leave to their God and to themselves.—They have, in pronouncing their verdict, thought proper to recommend me as an object of humane mercy; in return, I pray to God, if they have erred, to have mercy upon them. The Judge, who condemned me, humanely shed tears in uttering my sentence; but whether he did wisely, in so highly commending the wretched informer who swore away my life, I leave to his own cool reflection, solemnly assuring him and all the world, with my dying breath, that the informer was forsworn. The law under which I suffer, is surely a severe one; may the makers and promoters of it, be justified in the integrity of their motives and the purity of their own lives—by that law, I am stamped a felon, but my heart disdains the imputation. My comfortable lot and industrious course of life, best refute the charge of being an adventurer for plunder: but if to have loved my country, to have known its wrongs, to have felt the injuries of the persecuted Catholics, and to have united with them and all other religious persuasions, in the most orderly and least sanguinary means of procuring redress:— If those be felonies, I am a felon, but not otherwise. Had my counsel (for whose honorable exertions I am indebted) prevailed in their motion to have me tried for High-treason, rather than under the *Insurrection Law*, I should have been intitled then to a full defence, and my actions and intentions have been better vindicated; but that was refused, and I must now submit to what has passed.

To the generous protection of my country, I leave a beloved wife, who has been constant and true to me, and whose grief for my fate has aleady nearly occasioned her death. I leave five living children, who have been my delight—may they love their Country as I have done, and die for it, if needful.

Lastly, a false and ungenerous publication having appeared in a newspaper stating, certain alledged confessions of guilt on my part, and thus striking at my reputation, which is dearer to me than life, I take this solemn method of contradicting that calumny: I was applied to by the High-Sheriff, and the Rev. William Bristow, Sovereign of Belfast, to make a confession of guilt, who used entreaties to that effect; this I peremptorily refused; did I think myself guilty, I should be free to confess it, but, on the contrary, I glory in my innocence.

I trust, that all my virtuous countrymen will bear me in their kind remembrance, and continue true and faithful to each other, as I have been to all of them. With this last wish of my heart, not doubting of the success of that cause for which I suffer, and hoping for God's merciful forgiveness of such offences as my frail nature may have at any time betrayed me into, I die in peace and charity with all mankind.

WILLIAM ORR
Carrickfergus Gaol, October 5, 1797

THE PRESS, 17 OCTOBER 1797

VIVE LE REPUBLIC

November 1, 2, 3. My brother Matthew joined me from Hamburgh, where he arrived about a month ago. It is a great satisfaction to me, and I hope he arrives just in time to take a part in the expedition . . .

November 20. Yesterday General Hédouville presented me to Desaix, who is arrived within these few days. I could not possibly desire to meet a more favorable reception; he examined me a good deal as to the localities of Ireland, the face of the country, the facility of finding provisions; on which I informed him as well as I could. He told me that he had not directly the power himself, to name the officers who were to be employed in the army of England, but that I need not be uneasy, for I might rely I should be of the number . . . So I may happen to have another offer at John Bull before I die. God knows how I desire it.

GENERAL BUONAPARTE

December 11, 12. Called this day, with Lewines, on General Desaix, and gave him Taylor's map of Ireland. He tells us to be under no anxiety; that the French Government will never quit the grip which they have got of England, till they humble her to the dust; that it is their wish, and their interest, (that of all France, as well as of Ireland,) that the Government now had means, and powerful ones, particularly money, and they would devote them all to this great object; it might be a little sooner or a little later, but that the success of the measure was inevitable . . .

December 18, 19, 20, 21. General Desaix brought Lewines and me this morning and introduced us to Buonaparte, at his house in the Rue Chantereine. He lives in the greatest simplicity . . . His face is that of a profound thinker, but bears no marks of that great enthusiasm and unceasing activity by which he has been so much distinguished . . . We told him that Tennant was about to depart for Ireland, and was ready to charge himself with his orders if he had any to give. He desired us to bring him the same evening, and so we took our leave. In the evening we returned with Tennant, and Lewines had a good deal of conversation with him; that is to say, Lewis *insensed* him a good deal on Irish affairs . . .

December 23. Called this evening on Buonaparte, by appointment, with Tennant and Lewines, and saw him for above five minutes. Lewines gave him a copy of the memorials I delivered to the Government in February, 1796, (nearly two years ago,) and which, fortunately, have been well verified in every material fact, by every thing that has taken place in Ireland since. He also gave him Taylor's map, and showed him half a dozen of Hoche's letters, which Buonaparte read over. He then desired us to return in two or three days, with such documents relating to Ireland as we were possessed of, and, in the mean time, that Tennant should postpone his departure. We then left him. His manner is cold, and he speaks very little; it is not, however, so dry as that of Hoche, but seems rather to proceed from languor than any thing else. He is perfectly civil, however, to us; but, from any thing we have yet seen or heard from him, it is impossible to augur any thing good or bad. We have now seen the greatest man in Europe three times, and I am astonished to think how little I have to record about him . . . Yet, after all, it is a droll thing that I should become acquainted with Buonaparte. This time twelve months, I arrived in Brest, from my expedition to Bantry Bay. Well, the third time, they say, is the charm. My next chance, I hope, will be with the *Armée d'Angleterre—Allons! Vive la Republique!*

A MAP
of
IRELAND
to
Elucidate the
IRISH REBELLION
of 1798

ATLANTIC OCEAN

SCALE
British Statute Miles
Irish Miles

LIST of the COUNTIES

Antrim	3	Limerick	
Armagh	7	Londonderry	
Carlow	28	Longford	
Cavan	12	Louth	
Clare	22	Mayo	
Cork	31	Meath	
Donegall	1	Monaghan	
Down	8	Queens	
Dublin	21	Roscommon	
Fermanagh	5	Sligo	
Galway	18	Tipperary	
Kerry	30	Tyrone	
Kildare	20	Waterford	
Kilkenny	27	Westmeath	
Kings	19	Wexford	
Leitrim	11	Wicklow	

1798

THE WIDOW

WAKE OF WILLIAM ORR

Here our worthy brother lies;
Wake not *him* with women's cries:
Mourn the way that manhood ought;
Sit in silent trance of thought.

Write his merits on your mind;
Morals pure and manners kind;
In his head as on a hill,
Virtue plac'd her citadel.

Why cut off in palmy youth?
Truth he spoke, and acted truth.
Countrymen UNITE, he cry'd,
And dy'd—for what his Saviour dy'd,

God of Peace, and God of love,
Let it not thy vengeance move,
Let it not thy lightnings draw;
A Nation guillotin'd by law.

Hapless Nation! rent, and torn,
Thou wert early taught to mourn,
Warfare of six hundred years!
Epochs marked with blood and tears.

Hunted thro' thy native grounds,
A flung *reward* to human hounds;
Each one pull'd and tore his share,
Heedless of thy deep despair.

Hapless Nation—hapless Land,
Heap of uncementing sand!
Crumbled by a foreign weight;
Or by worse, domestic hate.

God of mercy! God of peace!
Make the mad confusion cease;
O'er the mental chaos move,
Through it SPEAK the light of love.

Monstrous and unhappy sight!
Brothers blood will not unite;
Holy oil and holy water,
Mix, and fill the world with slaughter.

Who is she with aspect wild?
The widow'd mother with her child,
Child new stirring in the womb!
Husband waiting for the tomb!

Angel of this sacred place
Calm her soul and whisper peace,
Cord, or ax, or Guillotin'
Make's the sentence—not the sin.

Here we watch our brothers sleep,
Watch with us; but do not weep;
Watch with us thro' dead of night,
But expect the morning light.

Conquer fortune—persevere!—
Lo! it breaks, the morning clear!
The cheerful COCK awakes the skies,
The day is come—arise!—arise.

> Feminis lugere honestum est,
> Viris *meminisse*

THE PRESS, 13 JANUARY 1798

THE COMPLEXION OF THE TIMES

STRADBALLY (QUEEN'S COUNTY)

The complexion of the times is altered for the worse. This part of the country, hitherto peaceably inclined, was of a sudden disturbed by those nocturnal banditti called *Defenders* or *United Irishmen*. The families for six miles round us, are afraid to stir out of their houses, or to continue in them. Every morning brings fresh intelligence of depredations; and the plans are carried on with a degree of caution and secrecy that adds to the general astonishment.

THE TIMES, 5 FEBRUARY 1798

March 21 to 24. This day I received my orders to set off for head-quarters at Rouen, where I am to remain at the suite of the Etat Major, till further orders. There is at least one step made.

March 25. Received my letters of service from the War Office, as Adjutant General in the Armée d'Angleterre. This has a lofty sound to be sure, but God knows the heart! Applied to the Minister at War for leave to remain a few days in Paris, to settle my family, which he granted.

March 26. I see in the English papers of March 17th, from Irish papers of the 13th, news of the most disastrous and afflicting kind, as well for me individually as for the country at large. The English government has arrested the whole committee of United Irishmen for the province of Leinster, including almost every man I know and esteem in the city of Dublin. Amongst them are Emmet, M'Neven, Dr. Sweetman, Bond, Jackson, and his son; warrants are likewise issued for the arrestation of Lord Edward Fitzgerald, M'Cormick, and Sampson; who have not however yet been found.

JOURNALS OF THEOBALD WOLFE TONE, MARCH 1798

CONDUCT BEST CALCULATED FOR
OBTAINING VICTORY

If ever any unfortunate cause should put our city, with the other parts of the country, into the possession of a cruel and tyrannical enemy, whose government, by repeated oppressions, might drive us into the last stage of desperate resistance, our conduct then should be regulated in a manner best calculated for obtaining victory. The following thoughts are humbly offered for the inspection of every real Irishman:—

It is supposed that the enemy have a well-appointed and disciplined standing army.

In such a case every man ought to consider how that army could be attacked or repelled, and what advantage their discipline and numbers might give them in a populous city, acting in concert with the adjoining counties.

It is well known that an officer of any skill in his profession would be very cautious of bringing the best disciplined troops into a large city in a state of insurrection, for the following reasons:—

His troops, by the breadth of the streets, are obliged to have a very narrow front, and however numerous, only three men deep can be brought into action, which, in the widest of our streets, cannot be more than sixty men, as a space must be left on each side or flank, for the men who discharge to retreat to the rear, that their places may be occupied by the next in succession, who are loaded; so, though there are a thousand men in a street, not more than sixty can act at one time; and should they be attacked by an irregular body armed with pikes or such bold weapons, if the sixty men in front were defeated, the whole body, however numerous, are unable to assist, and immediately become a small mob in uniform, from the inferiority of number in comparison to the people, and easily disposed of.

Another inconvenience might destroy the order of this army. Perhaps at the same moment they may be dreadfully galled from the house-tops by showers of bricks, coping-stones, etc., which may be at hand, without imitating the women of Paris, who carried the stones of the unpaved streets to the windows and tops of the houses in their aprons.

Another disadvantage on the part of the soldiers would be, as they are regulated by the word of command, or stroke of the drum, they must be left to their individual discretion, as such communications must be drowned in the noise and clamour of a popular tumult.

In the next place, that part of the populace who could not get into the engagement, would be employed in unpaving the streets, so as to impede the movements of horse or artillery; and in the avenues where the army was likely to pass, numbers would be engaged forming barriers of hogsheads, carts, cars, counters, doors, etc., the forcing of which barriers by the army would be disputed, while like ones were forming at every twenty or thirty yards, or any convenient distances situation might require. Should such precautions be well observed, the progress of an army through one street, or over one bridge, would be very tedious, and attended with great loss, if it would not be destroyed. At the same time, the neighbouring counties might rise in a mass, and dispose of the troops scattered in their vicinity, and prevent a junction or a passage of any army intended for the city; they would tear up the roads, and barricade every convenient distance with trees, timber, implements of husbandry, etc., at the same time lining the hedges, walls, ditches, and houses with men armed with muskets, who would keep up a well-directed fire.

However well exercised standing armies are supposed to be by frequent reviews and sham battles, they are never prepared for broken roads or enclosed fields, in a country like ours, covered with innumerable and continued intersections of ditches and hedges, every one of which are an advantage to an irregular body, and may with advantage be disputed against an army, as so many fortifications and entrenchments.

The people in the city would have an advantage by being armed with pikes or such weapons. The first attack, if possible, should be made by men whose pikes were nine or ten feet long: by that means they could act in ranks deeper than the soldiery, whose arms are much shorter; then the deep files of the pikemen, by being weightier, must easily break the thin order of the army.

The charge of the pikemen should be made in a smart trot. On the flank or extremity of every rank, there should be intrepid men placed to keep the fronts even, that at closing every point should tell together; they should have, at the same time, two or three like bodies at convenient distances in the rear, who would be brought up, if wanting, to support the front, which would give confidence to their brothers in action, as it would tend to discourage the enemy; at the same time, there should be in the rear of each division, some men of spirit to keep the ranks as close as possible.

The apparent strength of the army should not intimidate, as closing on it makes its powder and ball useless; all its superiority is in fighting at a distance; all its skill ceases, and all its action must be suspended, when once it is within reach of the pike.

The reason of printing and writing this, is to remind the people of discussing military subjects.

COPY OF A PAPER FOUND IN THE WRITING BOX OF LORD EDWARD FITZGERALD ON
12 MARCH 1798

DEBATE IN THE LORDS ON THE
STATE OF IRELAND

March 26. The Earl of *Moira* said:—I rise in consequence of some observations which fell from a noble marquis (Downshire) in the debate of Thursday last . . .

A noble peer stated himself prepared to give a broad contradiction to the positions advanced by me in a former debate upon the present state of Ireland. Of every thing which I advanced in this House, I offered to bring evidence. I afterwards went over to Ireland, laid down the same positions, and offered the same proof . . .

It is proper, however, that I should restate my former positions, to enable the noble lord to reply to them distinctly. I asserted, in the first place, that many districts and whole provinces, were put out of the king's peace, and under military law; that the military, in many instances, committed with impunity the most inordinate excesses, and a great number of houses were burned, and the inhabitants driven from their former habitations; that the tocsin or curfew was sounded at nine o'clock at night, to oblige the peasantry to put out their fires and their candles; and that this was so rigorously executed as, in one instance particularly, and no doubt there were many others, to outrage every feeling of humanity. I asserted, that torture was applied in the exploded manner of piqueting, to oblige the miserable inhabitants not only to confess against themselves, but also to extort from them informations against others. I farther stated, that in consequence of these oppressions, the trade of the country was rapidly declining. All these statements I undertake now to prove by affidavits . . .

The Marquis of *Downshire* said:—I am exceedingly sorry that the state of Ireland should be subject of debate in this House, which certainly has no jurisdiction over the executive government of that country. Such discussions, without being capable of producing any good effect, may do a great deal of mischief. I had reason to regret my not being present at the time when the noble lord made the motion to which he has alluded. I could then have explained to him how much he was misinformed; and I am now ready to correct him upon that subject in any manner or in any place he may think proper . . . I hold his conduct, in this instance, to have been ill-judged and indiscreet. Having been for nine months myself engaged in the focus of rebellion, I may be allowed to have more direct information than it was within the reach of other noble lords to attain; and it was from that knowledge I spoke in contradiction to the noble earl. That the military in some cases were guilty of more excess and severity than the lovers of good order could wish, is not to be disputed, but what I asserted on a former night, and what, I still maintain, is, that these excesses were not committed by the authority and countenance of the executive government, who on every occasion took care that such misconduct should be restrained and punished. I also assert, that no

118 outrages were committed with the consent or knowledge of the officers; and of that I am enabled to speak with the more certainty, as I was engaged myself in that service, for which I am not sorry to have become an object of aversion to the United Irishmen ... The troops in Ireland committed some excesses; but it might be remembered that they had the greatest provocation, and that nothing could exceed the atrocious conduct of the United Irishmen. I mean not to go back from any measures I have taken, or any advice I have given; and I here aver, that I was one of the first to recommend to the Irish government the system of coercion against those traitors and rebels the United Irishmen ... The system of parliamentary reform and catholic emancipation is the thinnest disguise imaginable to the treason of the Irish rebels, whose efforts tend to disunite their country from the crown of Great Britain, and reduce it to a province of the French republic. With men of such designs and dispositions, no conciliatory measures could produce any good effect; and their atrocities are continually inflaming the minds of the soldiers.

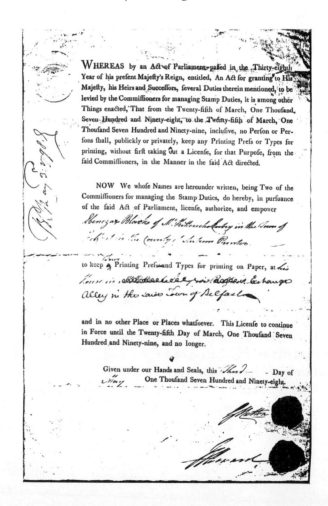

WHEREAS by an Act of Parliament passed in the Thirty-eighth Year of his present Majesty's Reign, entitled, An Act for granting to His Majesty, his Heirs and Successors, several Duties therein mentioned, to be levied by the Commissioners for managing Stamp Duties, it is among other Things enacted, That from the Twenty-fifth of March, One Thousand, Seven Hundred and Ninety-eight, to the Twenty-fifth of March, One Thousand Seven Hundred and Ninety-nine, inclusive, no Person or Persons shall, publickly or privately, keep any Printing Press or Types for printing, without first taking Out a License, for that Purpose, from the said Commissioners, in the Manner in the said Act directed.

NOW We whose Names are hereunder written, being Two of the Commissioners for managing the Stamp Duties, do hereby, in pursuance of the said Act of Parliament, license, authorize, and empower

to keep a Printing Press and Types for printing on Paper, at

and in no other Place or Places whatsoever. This License to continue in Force until the Twenty-fifth Day of March, One Thousand Seven Hundred and Ninety-nine, and no longer.

Given under our Hands and Seals, this ____ Day of ____ One Thousand Seven Hundred and Ninety-eight.

All who are acquainted with the dispositions of those rebels, are unanimous in the belief that coercion alone can produce any salutary effect
upon them. I never knew a Catholic of knowledge, or education, who
was a friend to what is termed, unqualified Catholic emancipation, nor
an enlightened Presbyterian, who was an advocate for radical reform . . .

There being no question before the House, the motion of adjournment was put and carried.

HANSARD'S PARLIAMENTARY DEBATES, 26 MARCH 1798

SO EASY A SITUATION

Whitehall, March 31, 1798

DEAR ROSS,

I have neither seen nor heard from any person belonging to Administration since I wrote to you yesterday, which affords me some
hopes that I shall escape the attack which I apprehended.

The Lord Lieutenant said in his letter to the Duke of P., that unless
some officer of high rank and estimation, and popular character, was
immediately sent, he considered the country to be in the most imminent
danger. Lord Spencer said to me, after reading the letter, You must go as
Lord Lieutenant, and Commander-in-Chief; I said, You are too good to
me, to wish to place me in so easy a situation . . .

Yours ever, most sincerely,

CORNWALLIS

MARQUIS CORNWALLIS TO MAJOR-GENERAL ROSS, 31 MARCH 1798

LIMERICK PROCLAIMED

The whole of the county Limerick, including the liberties of the
city of Limerick—and the baronies of Fermoy, Orrery, and
Kilmore, in the county of Cork, are proclaimed.

BELFAST NEWS-LETTER, 2 APRIL 1798

Sunday evening a Committee of United Irishmen were found sitting at the house of one *Magrath*, a Publican, and taken into custody. The Committee consisted of 11 members, and on their persons were found papers of the most treasonable nature, among others, a plan for co-operating with the mutiny in the event of a landing—an account of the arms, ammunition, &c. to be distributed by the Lieutenant-Colonels to the different Corps, and the form of a solemn Obligation to turn out whenever called upon, and to pay strict obedience to superior Officers. The prisoners were lodged in the Barracks of the Dumbarton Fencibles (the Old Custom-house), where they remain in custody. Their names are as follow:—John Dillon, James Reilly, Peter O'Brien, George Kerfoot, James Doyle, James Murphy, Thomas Dillon, James Karr, Joseph Donelly, John Kinselagh, and Roger Kane.

THE TIMES, 7 MAY 1798

ARREST OF LORD EDWARD FITZGERALD

This evening Lord EDWARD FITZGERALD was apprehended. He resisted the execution of the Secretary of State's warrant, and in consequence was much wounded. Captain RYAN, of a Yeomanry Corps, and Mr. Justice SWAN, to whom the warrant was entrusted, were also wounded; the former dangerously. Lord EDWARD has been committed to Newgate.

THE TIMES, 24 MAY 1798

CURFEW

The following NOTICE was distributed in Dublin on the 24th inst.

LIEUT. GEN. LAKE, commanding his Majesty's Forces in this kingdom, having received from his Excellency the Lord Lieutenant full powers to put down the Rebellion, and to punish Rebels in the most summary manner according to Martial Law, does hereby give notice to all his Majesty's subjects, that he is determined to exert the powers entrusted to him in the most vigorous manner for the immediate suppression of the same: and that all persons aiding in the present Rebellion, or in any wise aiding or assisting therein, will be treated by him as Rebels, and punished accordingly.

And Lieut. Gen. Lake hereby requires all the inhabitants of the City of Dublin (the great Officers of State, Members of the Houses of Parliament, Privy Counsellors, Magistrates, and military persons in uniform excepted) to remain within their respective dwellings from NINE o'clock at night till FIVE in the morning, under pain of punishment.

By order of Lieutenant General Lake,
Commanding his Majesty's Forces
in this kingdom,

G. HEWITT, ADJUTANT-GEN.

Dublin, Adjutant General's Office,
24th May, 1798

BELFAST NEWS-LETTER, 25 MAY 1798

The SHEARES's of Cork, were this day apprehended and committed for High Treason. On one of the two brothers a most treasonable paper was found. Mr. PATRICK BYRNE, of Grafton-street, an eminent bookseller, and two waiters of the Globe coffee-house, have likewise been apprehended.

THE TIMES, 26 MAY 1798

CAPTAIN SWAYNE

Whitehall, May 28, 1798

DEAR ROSS,

I was much disappointed when I called at your door yesterday at five o'clock, to find that you did not intend to come to town, although the reasons you give for deferring your journey are perfectly just . . .

Lady S. told me this morning that the accounts from Ireland were of the most alarming nature. Actual hostilities have been committed, and much blood spilt in and about Dublin. The Lord Lieutenant writes for troops, but from whence are they to come?

I am, in great haste, &c.,

CORNWALLIS

MARQUIS CORNWALLIS TO MAJOR-GENERAL ROSS, 28 MAY 1798

SAMUEL NEILSON

Martial law was proclaimed through the principal streets of this town on Sunday last.

Various persons were taken up on Sunday night and last night, and confined in the Market-house, for being found in the streets after Nine o'clock at night.

Some prisoners were also brought in to-day from Newtownards.

A car load of arms was yesterday brought into this Town from the County of Down.

This forenoon some concealed arms were found in a carpenter's stores in Donegall street.

Mr. Samuel Neilson of this Town, was taken up in Dublin on Wednesday last, on a charge of High-Treason, and committed to the New Prison.

BELFAST NEWS-LETTER, 29 MAY 1798

WAGGON BETWEEN BELFAST AND DUBLIN.

THE Public are respectfully informed, that a Waggon leaves Dublin, and one Belfast every week. Owing to some intended regulations, the Proprietor cannot for a short time fix certain days for their leaving either places; but the Public may depend on one going and coming every week. Goods left at the following places will be carefully and regularly forwarded by the Public's

Most Obedient and Obliged Servant,

May 28, 1795.   JAMES GRAHAM.

No. 5, Great Strand-street, Dublin.
Mr. Jaffey's, Drogheda.
Mr. Carragher's, Dundalk.
Mr. Quilton's, Newry.
Mr. Mooney's, Banbridge. Mr. Reilly's, Dromore.
Mr. Bradshaw's, Hillsborough.
Messrs. Logan and Palmer's, Lisburn.
Mr. M'Guickin's, Belfast.

FROM ANOTHER PAPER

Last night the Northern Mail Coach was stopped under Santry Wall, and, together with the letters it contained, burned. The circumstances were these: In a certain part of the road, cars were placed so as to obstruct the passage of the coach, which, having arrived at this point, was surrounded by nine or ten armed persons, who said that they intended no harm, but merely wished to prevent the contents of the mail from falling into the hands of a great body of insurgents, which was a little farther on. The coachman and guard conceiving by such language that their obstruction proceeded from loyal precaution,

N O T I C E

T O

B L A C K S M I T H S, &c. &c.

THE Chief Magistrates, and Principal Inhabitants of every Town, Village Parish, or Townland in the Northern District, are hereby instructed, that no Person will be permitted in future, on Pain of capital Punishment, to follow the Trade of Gunsmith, Armourer, Blacksmith, Whitesmith, or Manufacturer of any species of Metal, unless the most respectable Security is given for his good Conduct, and a Licence obtained from me, or any Officer of the Rank of a General or Field Officer, (being a Magistrate of the County,) at the nearest Post to the Place of such Person's Residence. If it shall be discovered that a Pikehead, or other offensive Weapon, shall have been made by any one procuring such Security, his Bail shall be forfeited, and the Offender, on Conviction, executed at his own Door. A Register of Persons, so Licenced, must be kept by such Chief Magistrates or Principal Inhabitants, to refer to on all Occasions A Copy of which is to be lodged with the Officer Commanding at the nearest Post

GEORGE NUGENT, Major General,
Commanding the Northren District.

Belfast, June 24th, 1798.

HANNA. Licensed Printer. ENNISKILEN.

made no resistance, and were undeceived only by seeing the coach, &c. in a few moments in flames, they having previously been forced into an adjoining house. In the fields, near to where the transaction took place, were assembled a large body of people, not less, as the mailcoachmen calculated, than 2 thousand persons. A small remnant of the letters were brought, half burnt, to the Post-office. None of the passengers were ill-treated, nor any thing taken from their persons. The Connaught mail was also stopped between Lucan and Leixlip, and broken to pieces, and the letters destroyed. The guard was severely wounded.

THE TIMES, 29 MAY 1798

SAFETY OF THE EMPIRE

Dublin Castle, May 31, 1798

Sir—I had the honour of receiving two despatches by the last mail, enclosing the information of R ...

The rebels still continue in force in the Counties of Wicklow, Wexford, Kildare, Carlow, Meath, and King's County; it is difficult to bring them to any decisive action. They commit horrid cruelties, and disperse as soon as the troops appear. Should the insurrection confine itself within the present limits, a short time will dispose of it. There are some unpleasant appearances in certain parts of the North, but as yet all is in fact quiet in Ulster, Munster, and Connaught ...

The spirit of the country rises with its difficulties. Should the rebellion prove only partial, aided by the reinforcements expected from England, I look with confidence to the issue, which, if fortunate, cannot fail to place this kingdom, and of course the empire, in a state of security much beyond that in which it has stood for years past.

I have the honour to be, &c.

CASTLEREAGH

LORD CASTLEREAGH TO MR. WICKHAM, 31 MAY 1798

Extract of a letter from Tullamore, in the King's County, dated May 29, 1798

"We have constant alarms here, some well-founded, others without foundation; however, the yeomanry are spirited, and hold themselves in readiness to meet and cut down rebels and defenders."

At Newtown Mount-Kennedy, on Tuesday morning, a party of the rebels fell upon the town: they were opposed by the army and yeomanry; the town was burned, and Mr Gore, the yeoman Captain, wounded; but the rebels were defeated with unusual slaughter.

Great devastations have been committed by the rebels in the County Wicklow. They have burned all the houses in Ballymore, except three. The Marquis of Downshire's beautiful hunting-lodge, at Blessington, which cost upwards of £4000 is demolished, and a handsome inn, built at his Lordship's expense. The Earl of Milltown's estate at Russborough, has been pillaged of sheep, lambs, &c. and his house of provisions.

Yesterday died, in consequence of the wounds he received in assisting to apprehend Lord Edward Fitzgerald, Daniel Frederick Ryan, Esq. Captain of the St. Sepulchre's corps.

BELFAST NEWS-LETTER, 5 JUNE 1798

REBELLION IN IRELAND

Dublin, June 5, 1798

The latest advices inform us that the rebels are in possession of the towns of Arklow, Wexford, and Gorey. It is hard to decide whether they have been most wanton in their spoliations of the property, or cruel in their outrages on the persons of the inhabitants. The first eruption in that county was manifested in the promiscuous massacre of all the Protestant families, whom vigilance or precaution had not withdrawn into Enniscorthy or Wexford. The most dreadful effort was made against the Clergy—the Rev. Mr. BURROWS, of Kyle, fell with all his infant family, before those savages who filled the ranks of treason. The Rev. Mr. TURNER, of Ballingale, a loyal and zealous

Magistrate, was destroyed in his parish church during Divine Service. The Rev. JOSHUA NUNN, the most benevolent, the most respected, the most beloved Clergyman of his diocese, helpless and unresisting, weak and enfeebled by sickness, has also had his murder added to our disgrace! The long and sad catalogue of murders committed within the range of 20 miles in the miserable county of Wexford, is too horrible for recital.

The Protestant inhabitants of Ferns, upon the first appearance of insurrection, retired in a body to Enniscorthy; in that town they were assailed by an innumerable host of rebels: they fought gallantly; but, aided by traitors in the town, the rebels prevailed.

THE TIMES, 11 JUNE 1798

THE NORTH

A letter has also been received from Major-General Nugent, at Belfast, dated the 9th instant, which states, that the rebels were dispersed in all directions, except at Toome, whither General Knox and Colonel Clavering were proceeding; and that many of them had laid down their arms. The Major-General also states, that Mr. M'Cleverty had returned from Donnegor-Hill, whither he had been carried prisoner by a body of 2000 rebels. Whilst they were in this station they disagreed and quarrelled among themselves, and from his influence—above fifteen hundred left the camp, broke and destroyed their arms, and swore they would never again carry an offensive weapon against his Majesty or his loyal subjects; many more dispersed, and the commander of them was left with fifty men only.

BELFAST NEWS-LETTER, 12 JUNE 1798

Dublin Castle, June 12, 1798

Private.

Sir—I am honoured this day with your letter of the 8th, the military intelligence of which will prove most acceptable on this side of the water. It is of importance that the authority of England should decide this contest, as well with a view to British influence in Ireland, as to make it unnecessary for the Government to lend itself too much to a party in this country, highly exasperated by the religious persecution to which the Protestants in Wexford have been exposed.

In that county, it is perfectly a religious phrensy. The priests lead the rebels to battle: on their march, they kneel down and pray, and show the most desperate resolution in their attack . . . They put such Protestants as are reported to be Orangemen to death, saving others upon condition of their embracing the Catholic faith. It is a Jacobinical conspiracy throughout the kingdom, pursuing its object chiefly with Popish instruments; the heated bigotry of this sect being better suited to the purpose of the republican leaders than the cold, reasoning disaffection of the northern Presbyterians. The number of the insurgents is great,—so great as to make it prudent to assemble a very considerable force, before any attempt is made to penetrate that very difficult and enclosed country . . .

I have the honour, &c.,

ps.—By accounts from the North today, there does not appear, as yet, any extension of the evil in that province. In some parts of Antrim, the principle of property, I suspect, rather than repentance, has induced a partial submission. Our information, which has hitherto proved most lamentably true, states that Down and Antrim are to move before the other Counties;—this has happened;—that the other Counties are to follow; and that the rising is to be general between the 11th and 20th. I hope for once we shall be deceived.

LORD CASTLEREAGH TO MR WICKHAM, 12 JUNE 1798

Through a conviction of my many improprieties, and as a sort of atonement for those transgressions, I lay this before the world; and should it but warn and save even one from the ruin that attends keeping improper company, and giving loose to his passions, I shall think myself highly rewarded for my trouble and exposure of my iniquities . . .

Of my father or mother, I shall not say more, than that they are both descended from Scotch families, who had fled from that country at the rebellion. I was the first fruit of their union, being born in Downpatrick on the 29th of June, 1771; from my earliest infancy, I shewed a propensity to mischief, and during my juvenile years practised every species of it, such as robbing of orchards, mitching, and barring out the master, &c. . . .

EDWARD NEWELL

On my arrival in Dublin, I gave myself up solely to the enjoyment of my companions two of them in particular whom I informed I had determined to leave my father's house, but had not as yet formed any plan to proceed upon . . . I therefore, went to take a passage for England, but on Rogerson's quay, I met Captain Johnson enlisting seamen to go to Spain. The thought struck me I should go see the world, as I had been always fond of the sea; though I had now an opportunity of gratifying myself, and living without my parents . . .

We sailed for Cadiz, and on the thirteenth night at sea, being very dark there arose a most dreadful storm, then did I first witness the dangers of the sea. About two o'clock in the morning, we came right aground, on a range of rocks at Cape St. Mary's, where after a scene of horrors, our boat being staved in attempting to gain the shore, and obliged to lie there sometime, we got off and performed our voyage.

During my stay in the ship, I made several voyages, viz. to Cape and Port St. Mary's, Port a Palos, and Parce Povelo, St. Lucia, Seville, and up the streights. From Cadiz I wrote to my father, giving him an account of my proceedings, &c. . . . After great exertions, we at length made the Irish coast, but from the encreasing tempest and our shattered state, we were forced to run for Holyhead . . .

After my return to Dublin, my father, commisserating my sufferings at sea, wished me to settle, and bound me to the painting and glazing business, which I reluctantly followed for a year . . .

Spouting in private theatres, and all its concomitant extravagancies was my constant delight, by such means and a connexion with a young woman I was reduced to the necessity of leaving Dublin with her, and went to Limerick, in order to proceed to Baltimore in America . . .

In Limerick I again attempted business, but was again unsuccessful, and therefore returned to Dublin . . . My parents to whom I applied, refused the smallest assistance on account of *my being a Defender* . . .

I know every honest man among you is highly and justly pre-possessed against me . . . To you—as to my God, will I open all my soul;—to you; shall I confess, that *anger* and *revenge* first made me a *villain*; and *luxury, ambition, false pride*, and *bribery* caused me for a while to *continue one*.

Like Bird I try not to screen myself from your contempt by vain pretences, by pretending still to have been *true* to you:—*No!* though I have been once deceitful—Here I drop the character . . .

How will your heart shudder, when I shall *confess plans* of *extermination* by *military law* and *perjury!* and that perjury supported by your *government*, by the supporters of our *glorious constitution!*

I own myself guilty of perjury; first, in taking the oath of a citizen of Ireland, then deserting;—then in swearing against *her friends* many false-hoods, and now again denying what I had sworn.

About the beginning of the year 1796, I was recommended to go to Belfast by a sincere friend; "There," said he, "you will find every man a lover of his country, there shall you be rewarded for your sufferings, by the number of friends you shall find attached to your cause!" I went to Belfast, after being sometime there I became an United Irishman . . .

My over warmth, my too great love of the cause, were construed into a plan to deceive; and I was looked upon as an agent of administration; my most anxious endeavours to promote, were looked upon as schemes to destroy UNION, and I at last fell a prey to ill judged suspicion . . .

132   I became acquainted with a Mr. MURDOCH, a hearth-money collector, to whose house I went to do some pictures; during the time I was treated with the utmost kindness and attention. I thought myself esteemed by the family, and they were *really so* by me . . .

Some friends of mine, who knew his character, who knew the secret villainy of his heart, laid a plan to rid the world of such a miscreant, and supply themselves with the arms with which his habitation abounded. I was admitted and sworn one of this association; and though sworn, yet such was my respect and attachment to the family, (for then I knew them not) that I apprised them of their danger, and recommended guards for the house.—In return *he* rewarded me by informing all he knew of my being a rebel as he called it, and an assassin.

Here then, the people thought, themselves justifiable in their suspicion; they thought, and they thought rightly, such a rascal should not be left alive. I had papers in my possession of some value, at the appointed time I appeared not as I should have done, to deliver up my trust, "because I was detained by illness;" fresh proof of perfidy in *their* eyes.

I apprehended my life was in danger, conscious of the innocence of my intentions, and exasperated at their suspicions of me I returned to Murdoch's house; ill-fated return, the cause of all my woes!

There, these blood thirsty cannibals, these fiends of Hell, took care to blow the spark of resentment which glowed within my breast until it became a blaze; and, when once fully heated, when once raised to desperation and revenge by their damned insinuations, they took care I should have no time to return to reason,—until they hurried me to the throne of despotism, to the chamber of seduction, to that arch betrayer of every honest heart, the diabolical agent of the sanguinary Pitt,—the damned insinuating COOKE.

When I arrived in Dublin, where Bob Murdoch accompanied me; we, having been provided with money and horses, by Robert Kingsmill, Esq. the cowardly commandant of the Castlereagh cavalry, who is an *honest* Orange-man, and to whom I gave information of the societies, which were afterwards taken at Alexander's. I was conducted to Mr. Cooke, by that old pander of iniquity, Col. Ross, *there* I met with all that sweetness of reception, that cringing servility, and fulsome flattery such sycophants ever use to those whom they wish to seduce to their own ends.

THE APOSTACY OF NEWELL, LONDON, 1798

LORD VISCOUNT O'NEILL   LORD MOUNTJOY

NEWS FROM THE NORTH

Dublin-Castle, June 12, 1798

Advices have been received from Major General Nugent, on the 9th instant, Colonel Stapelton had attacked a body of Rebels near Saintfield, and at first suffered some loss; but in a second attack he entirely defeated them, with great slaughter. Captain Chetwynd, Lieutenant Unite, and Ensign Sparks, were killed, and Lieutenant Edenfor wounded . . .

It appears that a Report which General Nugent had received of a large Body of Rebels having entrenched themselves near Toome-Bridge, is unfounded, a party of them, which had been dispersed, had broke down one of the arches. The bridge has been again made passable.

Colonel Clavering has reported from Antrim, to General Nugent, that the disaffected in the neighbourhood of Antrim had expressed a desire to submit and return to their duty. At Ballymena, one hundred and fifty muskets, and eight hundred pikes, have been given up to the Magistrates; many arms, five hundred pikes, and a brass field piece, have also been surrendered to Major Seddon.

General Nugent expresses his warmest acknowledgements to the Regulars, Militia and Yeomanry Force under his command, for their alertness, zeal, and spirit.

BELFAST NEWS-LETTER, 15 JUNE 1798

No. 1. Where the rebel columns from Ballyclare and Templepatrick joined.
2. The rebels in close column with a six-pounder in front, when the curricle guns under lieutenant Neville opened their fire on them.
3. Lieutenant Neville, with two six-pounders, flanked by the yeomanry and dragoons under colonel Lumley, firing on the rebels.
4. Colonel Lumley charging the rebels after passing the church-yard.
5. The church yard lined with rebels, who are represented by the dotted lines, firing on the dragoons, charging as they passed, and among whom they did great execution.
6. The guns under lieutenant Neville, after retreating from No. 3, firing on the second column of the rebels advancing up Bow-lane.
7. The second rebel column.
8. The dragoons, after charging, drawn up under the dead wall of lord Massareene's garden, and covered on their left flank by a demi bastion.
9. The yeomanry firing over the wall on the rebels who attempted to get possession of the guns at No. 6, after the artillery had abandoned them, and the dragoons had retreated across the river.
10. The watering-place over which the dragoons retreated.
11. The entrance to Lord Massareene's court; the dotted lines from it represent the road by which the yeomanry retreated to take post in the garden, where they could only be attacked by the narrow walk through which they got in.
12. Lord Massareene's castle.
13. Lord Massareene's demesne.
14. Lord Massareene's walled garden.
15. The Six-mile water.
16. Colonel Durham with the Monaghan militia, and capt. Coulson of the artillery, firing on the rebels retreating by the Ballymena road.
17. The light battalion from Blaris camp under colonel Clavering drawn up.
18. Distillery.
19. Barracks.
20. Doctor Macartney's house.
21. Flour-mills.
22. Market-house with the prisoners.
23. Little guard-house, behind which lord O'Neil was killed.
24. The rebel reserve column under colonel Orr.

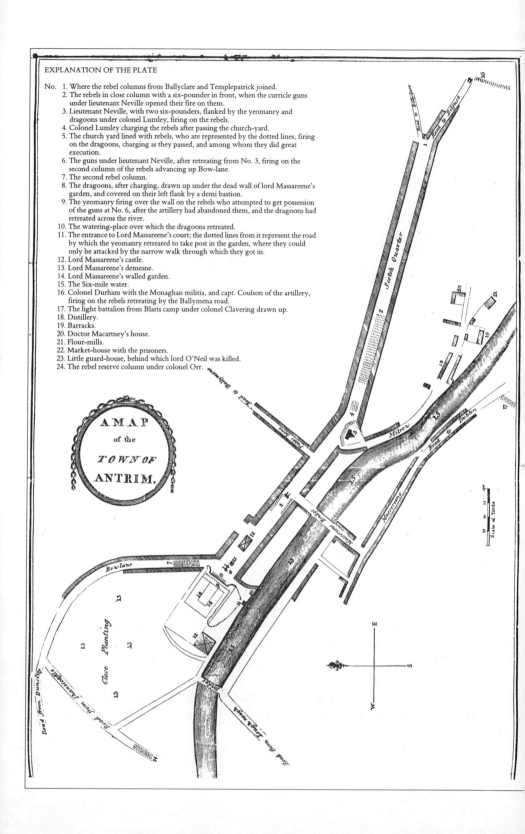

A MAP of the TOWN OF ANTRIM.

Whitehall, June 12, 1798

Dispatches of which the following are Coppies, have been received from his Excellency the Lord Lieutenant of Ireland by his Grace the Duke of Portland, his Majesty's Principal Secretary of State for the Home Department:—

Dublin Castle, June 9, 1798

MY LORD,

It is with the utmost concern I acquaint your Grace, an Insurrection has broken out in the county of Antrim; and in order to give your grace the fullest information in my power, I inclose to you an extract of a letter received this morning by Lord Castlereagh from Major-General Nugent. I am in great hope, from the numbers and spirit of the loyal in that part of the country, the Insurgents may be quickly checked. I have the honour to be, &c. &c.

CAMDEN

HIS GRACE THE DUKE OF PORTLAND

Belfast, June 8, 1798

MY LORD,

I have the honour to report to your Lordship, that in consequence of information, which I received early yesterday morning, of an intended Insurrection in the county of Antrim, having for its first object the seisure of the magistrates, who were to assemble that day in the town of Antrim, I apprehended several persons in Belfast. I did not receive the intelligence early enough to prevent the Insurgents from taking possession of Antrim, and I am not therefore acquainted with their first proceedings there; but I prevented many magistrates from leaving Belfast; and many others, being officers of Yeomanry on permanent duty, did not attend the meetings. I ordered the 64th Regiment, and light battalion, and 100 of the 22nd Light Dragoons, under Colonel Clavering and Lieutenant Colonel Lumley, with two $5\frac{1}{2}$ inch howizers, and two curricle six-pounders, to proceed with the utmost dispatch through Lisburn to Antrim. I also ordered from the garrison 250 of the Monaghan Militia, with Lieutenant-Colonel Ker, and 50 of the 22nd Dragoons, together with the Belfast Yeomanry Cavalry, with Major Smith, to proceed under the command of Colonel Durham, with two curricle six-pounders, through Carmoney and Templepatrick to

Antrim, to co-operate with the other detachment. The dragoons under Lieutenant-Colonel Lumley, having made the attack upon the town without waiting for the light battalion, were fired upon from the windows of the houses, and were consequently obliged to retreat, with the loss of, I am sorry to add, three officers of that excellent regiment killed and wounded, and the two curricle six-pounders. Colonel Clavering, on his arrival near Antrim, finding the Rebels pouring into that town in great force, very judiciously took post on a hill on the Lisburn side, and reported his situation to M. General Goldie. In the mean time, Colonel Durham, with his whole detachment, proceeded to within half a mile of Antrim, and, after a cannonade of half an hour, drove the Insurgents completely out of the town, and retook the two curricle guns, together with one brass six-pounder, very badly mounted, of which, it seems, the Rebels had two, supposed to have been smuggled out of Belfast. The Colonel then proceeded, without the loss of a man, through the town (which, for obvious reasons, suffered much) to Shane's Castle and Randlestown, in which direction the principal part of the Rebels fled. He remains there still for orders from me.

BELFAST NEWS-LETTER, 18 JUNE 1798

NEWS OF THE LAST IMPORTANCE

*J*une 17, 18. The news I have received this morning, partly by the papers, and partly by letters from my wife and brother, are of the last importance. As I suspected, the brave and unfortunate Fitzgerald was meditating an attack on the capital, which was to have taken place a few days after that on which he was arrested. He is since dead in prison; his career is finished gloriously for himself, and, whatever be the event, his memory will live forever in the heart of every honest Irishman. He was a gallant fellow. For us, who remain as yet, and may perhaps soon follow him, the only way to lament his death is to endeavour to revenge it. Among his papers, it seems, was found the plan of the insurrection, the proclamation intended to be published, and several others, by which those of the leaders of the People, who have thus far escaped, have been implicated, and several of them seized. Among others, I see Tom Braughall, Lawless, son of Lord Cloncurry, Curran, son of the Barrister,

Chambers and P. Byrne, printers, with several others, whom I cannot recollect. All this, including the death of the brave Fitzgerald, has, it appears, but accelerated matters; the insurrection has formally commenced in several counties of Leinster, especially Kildare and Wexford ... At Monastereven, Naas, Clain, and Prosperous, the three last immediately in my ancient neighborhood, there have been skirmishes, generally, as is at first to be expected, to the advantage of the army; at Prosperous, the Cork militia were surprised and defeated. The villains—to bear arms against their country. Killcullen is burnt; at Carlow, four hundred Irish, it is said, were killed; at Castledermot, fifty; in return, in County Wexford, where appears to be their principal force, they have defeated a party of six hundred English, killed three hundred, and the Commander, Colonel Walpole, and taken five pieces of cannon. This victory, small as it is, will give the people courage, and show them that a red coat is no more invincible than a grey one. At Rathmines, there has been an affair of cavalry, where the Irish had the worst, and two of their leaders, named Ledwich and Keogh, were taken, and, I presume, immediately executed ...

From the blood of every one of the martyrs of the liberty of Ireland, will spring, I hope, thousands to revenge their fall... What will the French Government do in the present crisis? After all, their aid appears to be indispensable: for the Irish have no means but numbers and courage ...

June 20. To-day is my birth-day. I am thirty-five years of age; more than half the career of my life is finished, and how little have I yet been able to do ... I had hopes, two years ago, that, at the period I write this, my debt to my country would have been discharged, and the fate of Ireland settled for good or evil. To-day it is more uncertain than ever. I think, however, I may safely say, I have neglected no step to which my duty called me, and, in that conduct, I will persist to the last.

UNITED IRISHMEN IN TRAINING

JUST OBJECTS OF PUNISHMENT

Dublin Castle, June 22, 1798

Sir—I have had the honour of receiving your despatch dated Enniscorthy, the 21st June, which I have laid before the Lord-Lieutenant . . .

I consider the rebels as now in your power, and I feel assured that your treatment of them will be such as shall make them sensible of their crimes, as well as of the authority of Government. It would be unwise, and contrary, I know, to your own feelings, to drive the wretched people, who are mere instruments in the hands of the more wicked, to despair. The leaders are just objects of punishment . . .

I need not add more. The Lord-Lieutenant will himself convey to you his sentiments.

LORD CASTLEREAGH TO LIEUTENANT-GENERAL LAKE, 22 JUNE 1798

Wexford, June 23, 1798

My Lord—I have every reason to think matters will be settled shortly to the satisfaction of Government. I believe we shall have most of their generals. Roach has been tried this day, and will be executed, as will Keugh, who was both general, adviser, governor of the town, &c. I really feel most severely the being obliged to order so many men out of the world; but I am convinced, if severe and many examples are not made, the Rebellion cannot be put a stop to. I believe Cooke knows a good deal of Keugh. I am in great hopes of catching Bagnell Hervey. A Mr. Grogan, a man of £6000 per annum, is just brought in; what there is against him I don't exactly know; I imagine sufficient to convict him. It has been suggested to me that the surest mode to prevent people in such circumstances concerning themselves in these acts of violence would be to forfeit their estates; but, as I have no wish to visit the sins of the fathers upon the children, I shall not think of proposing such an act, but wait your orders upon the subject.

I will beg you to forward the enclosed to Lord Camden, whose departure I most sincerely regret for every reason, and particularly so as I think he would have enjoyed seeing an end to the Rebellion—a time which, in my opinion, is not far off.

I hope all things are going on well about Dublin. I suppose Sir James Stewart has given in his resignation: he seems very angry with me.

Yours faithfully

G. LAKE

LIEUTENANT-GENERAL LAKE TO LORD CASTLEREAGH, 23 JUNE 1798

THE GUILT OF PARTICIPATING IN THE WEXFORD REBELLION

We have, as long as possible, refrained from sanctioning those rumours which attached to several names the guilt of participating in the Wexford Rebellion: that of Mr. *Bagenal Harvey* was really mentioned; and, though we had the strong evidence of his having been an active and zealous Member of the infamous

Society of United Irishmen in aid of the report, we could not till this moment venture to make it public. The names of the other persons have been publicly mentioned; we are sorry to say, with nearly the same claim to credit, a Mr. *Samuel Cooper*, an Attorney, is said to have countersigned Counsellor Bagenal Harvey's summons to the town of Ross, as Secretary of the Army; Mr. *Mathew Keugh* (an half-pay Officer), who had risen from the meanest rank in the King's army to the Commission of Captain, and who some years ago was struck out of the Commission of the Peace for misconduct, is mentioned as Lieutenant-General. Mr. *William Talbot*, of Castle-Talbot, is, to our astonishment, spoken of: Mr. *Hughes*, of Ballytrant; Mr. *Edward Hay*, of Ballinkeel; Mr. *John Colclough*, of Balliteigue;—*Stafford*, of Skreene;— *Dixon*, of Castlebridge, and a number of others, principal Roman Catholics of that County, are mentioned without hesitation as the Chief Leaders.

THE TIMES, 23 JUNE 1798

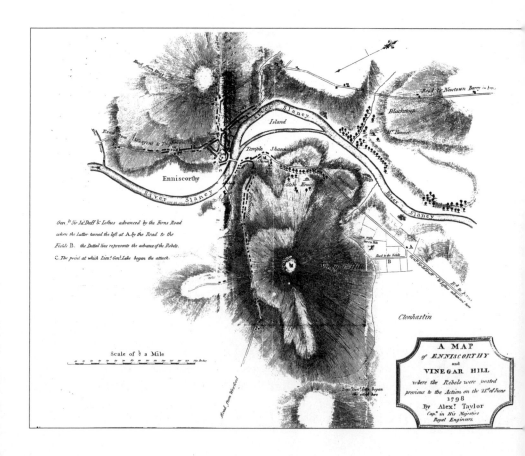

Yesterday another Mail arrived from Dublin, with letters of the 20th inst. By them we learn that Marquis CORNWALLIS arrived there on the evening of that day. He was received on his landing by the 100th Regiment, lately sent from hence, and by many of the Volunteer Corps, who lined the streets as his Lordship passed to the Castle.—Soon after his arrival there, a Council met, when the Noble Marquis was sworn into office, as Governor General and Commander in Chief.

In the North, there has been another trifling action near *Portaferry*, in which the Rebels were completely routed. According to letters received yesterday from Belfast, the rebellion in that part of the country is considered to be completely crushed.

THE TIMES, 25 JUNE 1798

HENRY MUNRO

In the County of Wexford, many hundreds of Rebels have been seized endeavouring to escape by sea; and every hour numbers of deluded Rebels throw themselves upon the mercy of the advanced posts of our army, in complete despair of any kind of success to their desperate designs.

We still continue to receive the most assuring accounts from the different parts of the kingdom in general. The south is perfectly tranquil, and the slight affair that took place at Roar, in the county of Kilkenny, was only occasioned by an incursion of the Wexford Rebels. Our letters from the North state, that the decided defeat which the insurgents sustained at Ballynahinch, promises to have effectually arrested rebellion in that quarter; and they further say, that the numbers of loyal persons making offers of military service, is beyond calculation.

THE TIMES, 25 JUNE 1798

UNITED IRISHMEN UPON DUTY

[Private.]

Dublin Castle, June 28, 1798

MY DEAR LORD,

The accounts that you see of the numbers of the enemy destroyed in every action, are, I conclude, greatly exaggerated; from my own knowledge of military affairs, I am sure that a very small proportion of them only could be killed in battle, and *I am much afraid that any man in a brown coat who is found within several miles of the field of action, is butchered without discrimination.*

It shall be one of my first objects to soften the ferocity of our troops, which I am afraid, in the Irish corps at least, is not confined to the private soldiers.

I shall immediately authorize the General Officers in the different districts which have been the seat of warfare, to offer (with certain exceptions) to the deluded wretches who are still wandering about in considerable bodies, and are committing still greater cruelties than they themselves suffer, the permission of returning quietly to their homes, on their delivering up their arms and taking the oath of allegiance, and I shall use my utmost exertions to suppress the folly which has been too prevalent in this quarter, of substituting the word *Catholicism* instead of Jacobinism, as the foundation of the present rebellion.

I have, &c.,

CORNWALLIS

MARQUIS CORNWALLIS TO THE DUKE OF PORTLAND, 28 JUNE 1798

THE VIOLENCE OF OUR FRIENDS

Dublin Castle, July 1, 1798

DEAR ROSS,

You see that our success has hitherto been almost uninterrupted, and if we can defeat or disperse a party of the vagabonds who are assembled in the Wicklow Mountains, I think our civil war will, for the present, be nearly at an end, but we shall have made no progress towards permanent peace ...

The violence of our friends, and their folly in endeavouring to make it a religious war, *added to the ferocity of our troops who delight in murder*, most powerfully counteract all plans of conciliation.

The life of a Lord-Lieutenant of Ireland comes up to my idea of perfect misery, but if I can accomplish the great object of consolidating the British Empire, I shall be sufficiently repaid.

I am interrupted. God bless you.

Believe me, &c.,

CORNWALLIS

MARQUIS CORNWALLIS TO MAJOR-GENERAL ROSS, 1 JULY 1798

A STATE OF *PRESENT* INACTIVITY

[Private and Confidential.]

Dublin Castle, July 8, 1798

MY LORD,

I not only wish to take the earliest opportunity of giving every light to His Majesty's confidential servants on the present state of our affairs, but to put them in possession of the best opinions which I have yet been able to form for extricating this country from the immediate danger with which it is threatened.

No actual force at this moment exists in arms against us, except in the county of Wicklow and the northern boundary of Wexford, and in the county of Kildare, and borders of the counties of Meath and Dublin.

In the former the Rebels act sometimes in small parties, but often in a considerable body, amounting, I believe (after due allowance for exaggeration) to at least five thousand men, the greater part of whom are armed only with pikes: the difficulty of coming up with an army of this kind without artillery and baggage, in that wild and mountainous country, has hitherto prevented our striking any serious blow, and the ignorance of our officers who have commanded small detachments, has afforded the Rebels some encouraging advantages; I am however at present arranging a plan of attacking them, which I hope will succeed so far as to disperse them, and to intimidate them so much as to prevent their assembling again in great numbers, which will to a certain degree have its effect in encouraging our friends and disheartening our enemies throughout the whole country; but I am not so sanguine as to hope to reduce the county of Wicklow to a peaceable state in a short time by force of arms.

The warfare in Kildare and the adjoining border of Meath is conducted on the part of the enemy entirely by small parties, which attack escorts and detachments, burn houses, murder those who will not join them, and retire to the bogs.

The rest of Ireland may, I am afraid, be rather said to be in a state of *present* inactivity than of any friendly or even peaceable intentions towards us.

The Irish militia are totally without discipline, contemptible before the enemy when any serious resistance is made to them, but ferocious and cruel in the extreme when any poor wretches either with or without arms come within their power; in short murder appears to be their favourite pastime.

Under these circumstances I conceive it to be of the utmost advantage that we should put an end to hostilities, provided that measure can be effected by the submission, delivery of arms, and apparent penitence of the Rebels, who have been defeated in every action of consequence, who have lost many leaders by the hands of the executioner, and who, from all accounts, are in general heartily tired of the business in which they are engaged.

The proclamation circulated by the Generals commanding in those districts which either are or have been in a state of insurrection, has, by the reports which I have received, been attended with considerable effect, but it has been represented to me that the greater number dare not desert their leaders, who have it in their power to destroy them if they should return to their houses, and these leaders are rendered desperate, by not having a hope held out to them that even their lives would be spared.

The term leader is indefinite, and it would not be easy to substitute any other denomination of persons for proscription, that would not, at least to the feelings of a guilty conscience, include every factious agitator of the present times.

In the proclamation of general pardon throughout the country, which I have now asked leave from His Majesty to issue (with the full approbation and concurrence of the Chancellor) I propose to exclude from security of life, only those who have been guilty of cool and deliberate murder, and to leave the leaders liable to banishment for such term as the safety of the state may require, to be extended in some instances to banishment for life; and it is proposed, after the report of a Secret Committee shall have been received, to require the surrender of three or four of the most dangerous persons, who are now supposed to be out of the country, within a reasonably limited time under pain of an Act of Attainder . . .

I should be very ungrateful if I did not acknowledge the obligations which I owe to Lord Castlereagh, whose abilities, temper, and judgment, have been of the greatest use to me, and who has on every occasion shown his sincere and unprejudiced attachment to the general interests of the British Empire.

I have, &c.,

CORNWALLIS

MARQUIS CORNWALLIS TO THE DUKE OF PORTLAND, 8 JULY 1798

HENRY JOY McCRACKEN

On Tuesday last came on the trial of H. McCracken.

The Court being duly sworn before the Prisoner he was informed he was to be tried for Treason and Rebellion, and for being in arms at Antrim on 7th June. The prisoner pleaded Not Guilty. The witnesses were examined whose evidence corroborated the above charge.

Being found guilty by the court—at five o'clock the prisoner was brought from the Artillery Barracks to the place of execution. Having been attended in person by a Clergyman, he was only a few minutes from the time he came out, till he was launched into eternity. After hanging one hour, his body was given over to his friends.

BELFAST NEWS-LETTER, 20 JULY 1798

EXECUTION OF THE MESS. SHEARES

Twelve o'clock on Saturday last having been appointed for the execution of these two unhappy men, when that hour passed by, and that the melancholy event did not take place, a belief became very general, that a respite had been given to them, and this opinion was strengthened by various reports actually to that effect, some making the period of respite 8, and others 14, days; the true cause of the delay is, however, said to have been applications made by these unfortunate gentlemen for a conditional protraction of their existence—which applications having been rejected by Government, they were launched into eternity about three o'clock.

The whole of the time immediately previous to this awful termination of their existence, was spent in spiritual

HENRY SHEARES

JOHN SHEARES

communication with the Rev. Doctor Dobbyn, of Finglas, and the Rev. Mr Gamble, Ordinary of Newgate. Both of them received the sacrament of the Lord's Supper. Henry Sheares is said to have professed on the scaffold, that his political views were confined to a Reform in Parliament—and in that declaration, and an abhorrence of indiscriminate massacre, he was joined by his brother John. The latter is also said to have uttered these words, "I hope this example will have the desired effect, but I much fear it will not: Government little know whom they ought to execute." We confess that our authority for these words of John Sheares, or the applications which he and his brother are said to have made to Government, is not the most respectable or impartial. The last words of Mr John Sheares were—"I forgive the world as I expect to be forgiven!"

After decapitation, the trunks and heads of both were delivered to their friends, and interred in St. Michan's church-yard.

The High Sheriffs testified the utmost consideration and humanity on this melancholy occasion.

BELFAST NEWS-LETTER, 20 JULY 1798

NO LAW BUT MARTIAL LAW

Dublin Castle, July 24, 1798

DEAR ROSS,

The overt rebellion is certainly declining, and the principal leaders in Kildare have surrendered with a stipulation for their lives only ... Except in the instances of the six state trials that are going on here, there is no law either in town or country but martial law, and you know enough of that to see all the horrors of it, even in the best administration of it, judge then how it must be conducted by

Irishmen heated with passion and revenge. But all this is trifling compared to the numberless murders that are hourly committed by our people without any process or examination whatever. The yeomanry are in the style of the Loyalists in America, only much more numerous and powerful, and a thousand times more ferocious. These men have saved the country, but they now take the lead in rapine and murder. The Irish militia, with few officers, and those chiefly of the worst kind, follow closely on the heels of the yeomanry in murder and every kind of atrocity, and the Fencibles take a share, although much behindhand with the others. The feeble outrages, burnings, and murders which are still committed by the Rebels, serve to keep up the sanguinary disposition on our side; and as long as they furnish a pretext for our parties going in quest of them, I see no prospect of amendment.

The conversation of the principal persons of the country all tend to encourage this system of blood, and the conversation even at my table, where you will suppose I do all I can to prevent it, always turns on hanging, shooting, burning, &c., &c., and if a priest has been put to death the greatest joy is expressed by the whole company. So much for Ireland and my wretched situation.

Believe me, &c.,

CORNWALLIS

MARQUIS CORNWALLIS TO MAJOR-GENERAL ROSS, 24 JULY 1798

DOWNPATRICK ASSIZES

The following persons have been lately tried at Downpatrick:—Thomas Coulter, of Lecale, in the county of Down, farmer, was brought forward for trial the 10th day of July instant, he being charged with having the command in the Rebel army and forcing others to join it—After a trial which occupied the Court several days—the crime being clearly proved, he was sentenced to be hanged the 20th, which was put in execution.

Robert Heasty, tried on suspicion of being concerned in plundering the house of Rev. Mr. Clewlow, of Saintfield, and for stealing a prayer-book—found guilty.—Sentence 300 lashes.

John Skelly, of Creevy Tennant, farmer, tried for Treason, he having a command in the Rebel Army, and for seditious practice. Sentence, Death. Executed the 21st instant.

Thomas Townsley, of Balloo, for Treason—Pleaded Guilty—To be transported for life.

William Bishop and Thomas Bishop, both of Ballymorrie, parish of Killinchy, farmers, tried for Treason and seditious practices—Pleaded Guilty—To be transported for life.

BELFAST NEWS-LETTER, 27 JULY 1798

PORTRAIT OF AN IRISH CHIEF

TO SUBDUE THEM OR INVITE THEM
TO SURRENDER

Dublin Castle, July 28, 1798

DEAR ROSS,

The rebellion in Kildare is now, I think, perfectly at an end, and the appearance of insurrection which showed itself in Tipperary has subsided, and there are scarcely any Rebels left in arms, except some parties of plunderers in the Wicklow mountains, where it is very difficult to get at them. I shall send Moore and Lord Huntley with the 100th regiment, and some troops that can be depended upon, to try either to subdue them or invite them to surrender, for the shocking barbarity of our national troops would be more likely to provoke rebellion than to suppress it.

Believe me, &c.,

CORNWALLIS

MARQUIS CORNWALLIS TO MAJOR-GENERAL ROSS, 28 JULY 1798

THE TRADE OF HIGHWAYMEN

The rebels, now broken every where into marauding gangs, have resorted, as was foreseen, to the trade of highwaymen. Their very leaders are ashamed of them, and study nothing now but to effect their escape, and throw themselves on the mercy of Government.

THE TIMES, 31 JULY 1798

CARRICKFERGUS CASTLE

GENERAL COURT MARTIAL
AT CARRICKFERGUS

Saturday, John Queery and Gawen Watt, both of Belfast, were brought before a General Court Martial, at Carrickfergus, charged with Treason and Rebellion, in being in arms with the Rebels at Antrim, on the 7th of June last. Both prisoners pleaded Guilty—John Queery received sentence to be transported for life, and Gawen Watt for seven years.

BELFAST NEWS-LETTER, 10 AUGUST 1798

TO CHECK THE PROGRESS OF THE ENEMY

Dublin Castle, Aug. 25, 1798

MY LORD,

I have the honour to acquaint your Grace that advices have been this morning received from Brigadier-General Taylor, dated Sligo the 24th instant, by which it appears that the enemy had taken possession of Ballina early on that morning, and that the three frigates had quitted the Bay of Killala.

I am collecting with all possible speed such a force as I trust will be sufficient in a very few days to check the progress of the enemy.

I have the honour, &c.,

CORNWALLIS

MARQUIS CORNWALLIS TO THE DUKE OF PORTLAND, 25 AUGUST 1798

LORD LAKE

Tuam, Aug. 28, 1798, 5 o'clock A.M.

MY LORD,

I was so much distressed when I wrote yesterday that I was not able to express my feelings, which were then, and still are, most acute . . . I think it absolutely necessary to state for your Lordship's information that it is impossible to manage the militia; their whole conduct has been this day of action most shameful, and I am sorry to say that there is a strong appearance of disaffection, particularly in the Kilkenny, as Lord Ormonde has reported to me . . .

I have reason to apprehend the people of the country are flocking in to the French very fast, which will not be prevented unless they are beat shortly, which I should think might easily be done with any troops but those I have to deal with.

I have, &c.,

G. LAKE

LIEUTENANT-GENERAL LAKE TO MARQUIS CORNWALLIS, 28 AUGUST 1798

SO SHAMEFUL A ROUT

[Private.]

Dublin Castle, Sept. 1, 1798

DEAR SIR,

I guarded you last night from believing as authentic what I had picked up of the Castlebar affair. I have just seen General Lake's secretary, who has left him from illness, and was at the battle. He says we had about 1100 firelocks, and 9 guns, and a good position. The French he cannot consider to have amounted to 800. He saw no peasantry. They came along the road in one column; when they came within cannon-shot our guns stopped the column, they then deployed in an irregular manner to the right, and advanced in an excellent style—with great rapidity as sharp-shooters.

Had our line been steady, all was right; but when the French were 150 yards off the Longford began running off, and then the Kilkenny, &c., and there was no possibility of rallying. The men totally indifferent to their officers, and so shameful a rout he never saw.

What I wrote of our artillery is true, and of Lord Ormonde's and Lord Granard's personal good conduct, and of the good behaviour of the detachment of Lord Roden. We are all quiet here.

Believe me, &c.,

E. COOKE

EDWARD COOKE, ESQ., TO WILLIAM WICKHAM, ESQ., 1 SEPTEMBER 1798

QUIET IN THE NORTH

Enniskillen, September 4, 1798

My dear Hewett—I returned here last night from Sligo where, I hope, matters are pretty well arranged . . .

Commissary Goldrisk is . . . sent from hence to Ballyagh-dirreen, to receive General Lake's orders, and will establish himself at Sligo, if thought proper . . .

Everything continues perfectly quiet in the North. We shall be able to add to the establishment of the corps of Yeomanry, agreeably to Lord Castlereagh's letter, and that will preclude the necessity of arming corps of Orangemen, which I have discouraged as much as possible, the arms and ammunition not being more than sufficient to render the additional Yeomanry fit for the field. Neither is it wise to arm the Orangemen generally (which must be done, if you once begin) until the last extremity, and that, I trust, is not very near. The Catholics appear to be very loyal throughout the North.

Yours, my dear Hewett, &c.,

G. NUGENT

GENERAL NUGENT TO MAJOR-GENERAL HEWETT, 4 SEPTEMBER 1798

The following Manifesto has been transmitted from the County Mayo, and is said to be published there by the French General:—

"Health and Fraternity to the People of Ireland!

"The *Great Nation* has sent me to you with a Band of Heroes, to deliver you from the hands of Tyrants—Fly to our standards, and share with us the glory of subduing the world. We will teach you the arts of war, and to despise the low pursuits of toil and industry—You shall live on the spoils of war and the labours of others. The acquisition of wealth is the acquisition of misery, and the enjoyment of ease is inglorious: we have made all the nations we have conquered happy, by arresting their property; by applying it to the *common cause*, and consecrating it to the Champions of Liberty!—Property is a *common right*, belonging to the valour that seizes it. We have already destroyed the unaspiring tranquility of Switzerland! and the wealth and the power and bigotry, of Italy are no more! If then the justice of France has thus extended its reforming vengeance to *unoffending nations*, consider with how much more rigour it will visit you if you shall slight its benignity. Fly to our standard, and we will free you from *spiritual* as well as *temperal* subjection; we will free you from the fetters of *religion* and the frauds of *priest-craft*.—Religion is a bondage intolerable to free minds; we have banished it from our own country, and put down the grand imposter, the *Pope*, whose wealth we have sacrificed on the altar of *reason*. Fly to our standards, and we will break your connection with England; we will save you from the mortification of seeing yourselves under an invidious Government, and exalt you into the rank of those countries which now enjoy the benefits of French Fraternity. Let not the ties of *kindred*, the seductions of ease, or any unmanly attachment to the *comforts of life*, teach you to neglect this friendly call of your Countryman and Fellow Citizen.

"SURAZIN, GEN."

THE TIMES, 6 SEPTEMBER 1798

SURRENDER OF THE FRENCH GENERAL HUMBERT TO GENERAL LAKE

SURRENDER OF THE FRENCH

Dublin Castle, 9th September, 1798

Advices have been received this morning from St. Johnstown, the Head Quarters of the Lord Lieutenant, which bring the pleasing and satisfactory intelligence, that Lieutenant General Lake having come up with the enemy yesterday morning, entirely defeated them. The French have surrendered at discretion. The Rebels who had joined them were dispersed, and a great proportion killed or taken. Lord Roden's Dragoons, the third Battalion of Light Infantry, and the Armagh regiment, were principally engaged, and distinguished themselves very much. Major General Cradock is slightly wounded in the shoulder. No officer killed.

The Lord Lieutenant's column had advanced with such rapidity from Carrick-on-Shannon to St. Johnstown, as to have been enabled to stop

BELFAST NEWS-LETTER, 11 SEPTEMBER 1798

WITH REGARD TO FUTURE PLANS

[Secret and Confidential.]

Dublin Castle, Sept. 16, 1798

MY DEAR LORD,

The quick succession of important events during the short period of my Lieutenancy has frequently diverted my attention from the pursuit of that great question—How this country can be governed and preserved, and rendered a source of strength and power, instead of remaining an useless and almost intolerable burthen to Great Britain.

Your Grace will not be so sanguine as to expect that I am now going to tell you that I have succeeded in making this discovery. Sorry am I to say that I have made no further progress than to satisfy myself that a perseverance in the system which has hitherto been pursued, can only lead us from bad to worse, and after exhausting the resources of Britain must end in the total separation of the two countries.

The principal personages here who have long been in the habit of directing the councils of the Lords-Lieutenants are perfectly well-intentioned and entirely attached and devoted to the British connexion, but they are blinded by their passions and prejudices, talk of nothing but strong measures, and arrogate to themselves the exclusive knowledge of a country, of which, from their mode of governing it, they have, in my opinion, proved themselves totally ignorant.

To these men I have shown all civility and kindness in my power, and have done for them all ordinary favours which they have asked, but I am afraid that they are not satisfied with me, because I have not thrown myself blindly into their hands. With the Chancellor, who can with patience listen to the words *Papist* and *Moderation*, I have invariably talked on all public points which have occurred, and I have shown no marks of confidence to any other set of men, and have particularly given no countenance whatever to those who opposed the former Government. I have at all times received the greatest assistance from Lord Castlereagh, whose prudence, talents, and temper I cannot sufficiently commend . . .

With regard to future plans I can only say that some mode must be adopted to soften the hatred of the Catholics to our Government. Whether this can be done by advantages held out to them from an union with Great Britain, by some provision for their clergy, or by some modification of tythe, which is the grievance of which they complain, I will not presume to determine. The first of these propositions is undoubtedly the most desirable, if the dangers with which we are surrounded will admit of our making the attempt, but the dispositions of the people at large, and especially of the North, must be previously felt.

I am, &c.,

CORNWALLIS

MARQUIS CORNWALLIS TO THE DUKE OF PORTLAND, 16 SEPTEMBER 1798

BANDS OF LAWLESS DESPERADOS

We learn from the Papers and private letters brought by it, that there no longer exists in any quarter of the country an appearance of insurrection which can tend in the smallest degree to excite any serious apprehensions. We are, however, concerned to observe, that some parts, particularly the county of Wicklow, are infested with bands of lawless depredators. Notwithstanding the measures of precaution and vigilance taken by Government to secure the Rebel Leader *Holt*, this desperate ruffian still continues to elude the pursuit of the military. The banditti which he commands are considerably reduced in number, and are represented to be in the most wretched state, deprived of every resource, and compelled to take refuge in the mountains and those parts which are most difficult of access.

THE TIMES, 8 OCTOBER 1798

Grosvenor Square, October 16, 1798

My dear Lord—I have seen Mr. Pitt, the Chancellor, and the Duke of Portland, who seem to feel very sensibly the critical situation of our damnable country, and that the Union alone can save it. I should have hoped that what has passed would have opened the eyes of every man in England to the insanity of their past conduct, with respect to the Papists of Ireland; but I can very plainly perceive that they were as full of their popish projects as ever. I trust, and I hope I am not deceived, that they are fairly inclined to give them up, and to bring the measure forward unencumbered with the doctrine of Emancipation.

THE EARL OF CLARE, LORD CHANCELLOR OF IRELAND, TO LORD CASTLEREAGH,

16 OCTOBER 1798

GENERAL HUMBERT TO THE EXECUTIVE DIRECTORY

Quarters General, Castlebar, 11 Fructidor,
(August 28.)

I transmit you, Citizens Directors, a report of my operations since my arrival in Ireland.

4 Fructidor, Aug. 21.—The army was named "The Army of Ireland;" we afterwards came in view of the landing place of Bradhaven; but the winds being contrary, has not been possible for us to approach the shore this day.

5 Fructidor, Aug. 22.—The Division of frigates after struggling twelve hours against wind and current, has moored in the Bay of Killala, about three o'clock P.M. As the English flag was flying, we were visited by several persons of distinction, and some English officers, whose astonishment upon discovering who we were it is impossible to describe. At four o'clock a landing was ordered. Adjutant-General Sarrazin disembarked first at the head of the grenadiers.—I ordered him to march against Killala, of which he took possession with the bayonet. I appointed him General of Brigade on the field of battle.—The enemy was completely routed. From this post guarded by two hundred men, about twenty saved themselves by flight across the marches; the rest were either killed or taken. Almost all the prisoners requested to serve with us. I acquiesced with pleasure in their demand. The landing was completely effected by ten o'clock at night.

6 Fructidor, Aug. 23.—General Sarrazin reconnoitred Ballina, where he had a light skirmish, the Cavalry of the enemy retiring in full gallop more than two leagues.

7 Fructidor, Aug. 24.—I marched with the army against Ballina. General Sarrazin, at the head of the grenadiers and a battalion of the infantry, overthrew every thing that opposed his passage. Adjutant General Fontaine was charged to turn the enemy; his attack was very successful, and he made several prisoners. I pursued the cavalry a long time with the brave soldiers of the third regiment of Chasseurs on horseback.

8 Fructidor, Aug. 25.—The French army was joined by a body of United Irishmen, who were immediately armed and cloathed. About eight o'clock at night I advanced to Rappa, and maintained that post until two.

—The army marched to Ballina, where it took a
position. It set out from thence at three o'clock P.M. After a march of
fifteen hours I arrived on the 10th Fructidor (Aug. 27.) at six in the
morning, on the heights at the back of Castlebar. I reconnoitred the
position of the enemy, which was very strong. I ordered General
Sarrazin to begin the attack. Some unskilful skirmishes were quickly
repulsed; the Chief of Battalion, Dufour, pursued them to the very foot
of the position of the enemy's army. The grenadiers advanced to the
charge in line of battle; the infantry of the line followed; the columns
formed under a fire of twelve pieces of cannon. Then General Dufour
attacked the left of the enemy with a battalion of the line, which was
obliged to fall back, exposed to the fire of more than two thousand
men. General Sarrazin flew to its assistance, at the head of the grenadiers,
and repulsed the enemy. The English kept up for about half an hour a
terrible fire of musquetry. General Sarrazin forbore answering it.—Our
fierce aspect disconcerted the English General. When the whole army
arrived, I ordered a general attack. General Sarrazin, at the head of the
grenadiers, overthrew the right of the enemy, and took three pieces of
cannon. The Chief of Battalion, Ardouin, forced their left to fall back
into Castlebar.

The enemy, concentrated in the town, and supported by their artillery, kept up a terrible fire. The 30th regiment of chasseurs charged in
the High Street of Castlebar, and drove the enemy beyond the bridge.
After several very bloody charges of both cavalry and infantry, led on by
General Sarrazin, and Adjutant General Fontaine, the enemy were
driven from all their positions, and pursued for more than two leagues.
The enemy lost 1800 men, of whom 600 were killed or wounded, and
1200 taken prisoners, besides ten pieces of cannon, five stand of colours,
1200 muskets, and almost all their baggage and stores. The standard
belonging to the enemy's cavalry has been given in charge to General
Sarrazin, whom I appointed General of Division on the field of battle. I
also appointed during the action, Adjutant General Fontaine, General of
Brigade; the Chiefs of Battalion, Azemard, Ardouin, and Dufour,
Chiefs of Brigade, Captain Dnrivak, Chief of a Squadron; and Captains
Touffaint, Zimmerman, Raccou, Huete, Babbin, and Ruty, Chiefs of
Battalion. I beg, Citizens Directors, that you will confirm these appoint-
ments, and expedite the brevets with all possible dispatch, as it will pro-
duce the very best effect. The officers and soldiers have all performed
prodigies. We have to regret, some excellent officers and brave soldiers
. . . I shall shortly send you further details. It is sufficient to inform you

that the army of the enemy, from five to six thousand men strong, of whom six hundred were cavalry, has been totally defeated.

Health and respect,

(Signed)   HUMBERT

BELFAST NEWS-LETTER, 20 OCTOBER 1798

FOUR FRIGATES AND A BRIG

Dublin, Oct. 29, 1798

DEAR ROSS,

When I thought that we were laid up quietly for the winter, behold another French armament in Killala Bay. We have different accounts of the number of their ships, but a lieutenant of the navy, who commands a cutter, reports the force to be four frigates and a brig, which latter was within hail, and fired at him. I should doubt whether they will land when they hear of the disaster of the former squadron.

Believe me, &c.,

CORNWALLIS

MARQUIS CORNWALLIS TO MAJOR-GENERAL ROSS, 29 OCTOBER 1798

THE HOCHE IN TOW OF THE DORIS

We hope to be able by next publication to give our Readers an account of the capture of the French squadron which appeared off Killala, it being next to impossible they could escape from our various cruizers in the quarter. The following letter from Dublin, mentioning that a cannonading was heard off Castlebar, confirms our opinion that we must soon have an account of them being captured.

Extracts of a letter from Dublin, dated Nov. 3.

"A report is prevalent that another engagement, off Killala, has taken place. I had a letter from Castlebar, which mentions, that a heavy cannonading was heard there for three hours without intermission."

Saturday the Marquis of Hertford and suite sailed for Portpatrick, on board of the Hillsbrough Packet.

It is with pleasure we announce to our readers the arrival of *La Hoche* in Lough Swilly on Wednesday evening last, in company with the *Robuste, Ethalion* and *Doris*. She has on board the well-known Theobald Wolfe Tone, and a number of Irishmen, emissaries of the Union, who are now in a likely way to pay the forfeit of their treasons. They have all been sent to Dublin.

BELFAST NEWS-LETTER, 6 NOVEMBER 1798

THE HEADS OF THE TREATY OF UNION

[Secret and Confidential.] Received Nov. 16, 1798

Whitehall, Nov. 12, 1798

MY LORD,

I have the honour of sending your Excellency inclosed, the heads of a Treaty of Union between this kingdom and Ireland, in which the King's confidential servants are of opinion that all the great interests of that country have been so fully and impartially attended to, that no material difficulty can occur in the completion of that measure, the necessity of which must be now no less apparent than its advantages.

I shall reserve for a separate letter such suggestions as I conceive your Excellency will expect to receive from hence, respecting the manner in which it may be wished that the outlines which are herewith communicated to you should be filled up, and they shall be accompanied by such observations and explanations as they may seem to require. But as I understand that the question of a Union is become a very general subject of discussion, and that consequently the friends of Government must be anxious to know the ideas as well as the wishes of Administration upon it, I have determined to transmit this plan to your Excellency, that you may be enabled, without further loss of time, to satisfy the expectations of your friends, and to bring forward the measure in such a manner as you shall judge most likely to facilitate and insure its success.

The heads of the Treaty of Union inclosed in the foregoing despatch of the Duke of Portland are, substantially, as follow:—

1. The kingdoms to be united, and the succession to remain as fixed by the existing laws.
2. The British Parliament to be unchanged. The Irish portion to be settled by an Irish Act.
3. Irish Peers to enjoy the same privileges as Scotch Peers.
4. All members of the United Houses to take the oaths now taken by British members; but such oaths to be subject to such alterations as may be enacted by the United Parliament.
5. The continuance of the present Irish Church Establishment to be a fundamental article of the Union.
6. Tariff in the French treaty of commerce with England in 1786, to be adopted as between England and Ireland. The duties may be diminished, but may never be increased. Countervailing duties to be enacted. Special provisions to be made with reference to the export of salt provisions and linen to Great Britain and to the Colonies.
7. Revenue and debts. The accounts to be kept separate. Ireland to pay —— of the annual charges. If the Irish taxes already existing produce a larger sum than the foregoing proportion, the surplus to be employed in paying off Irish debt.
8. The Courts of Justice to be untouched. Final appeal to the House of Lords.
9. The Great Seal of England to remain; so, also, the Privy Council

in Ireland, or else a Committee of Privy Council in Ireland. The
Lord-Lieutenant to remain, but not to be mentioned in the Act.

I have, &c.,

PORTLAND

THE DUKE OF PORTLAND TO MARQUIS CORNWALLIS, 12 NOVEMBER 1798

THEOBALD WOLFE TONE

The trial of T.W. Tone, by a Court Martial at the Barracks of
Dublin, of which General Loftus was president, concluded on
Saturday last.

Tone being asked whether he was
guilty or not of the charge of *having as a
false Traitor entered into the service of the
Enemy and appeared in arms against his Sovereign?* replied, that he would give the Court
no trouble, that he fully admitted the
charge.

He then read a kind of defence, in doing
which he was at three different inflammatory passages stopped by the Court, and
suffered to erase the obnoxious parts out
of the paper.

The general tendency of this paper was,
that he confessed having entered into the
French service; (and he produced his
Commission of *Chêf de Brigade*); that he
had embarked in the great design of raising Three Millions of his fellow-subjects
from a state of bondage; that he had made
the same attempt in which Washington
had succeeded, and Kosciusko had failed;
to the Catholics of Ireland he acknowledged his obligations, he had engaged sincerely in their service, and had been amply
remunerated; the connection of Ireland

THEOBALD WOLFE TONE

with Great Britain he had ever considered as her bane, and he had acted under that conviction to rescue his country; success he could not command, and he was prepared to meet his fate.

As a soldier, however, he wished to die like a soldier; he wished as an emigrant taken in arms, to be treated as the French had treated the Count de Sombrieul, and to be shot; the sooner his fate was to take place, the better; he wished it might be within an hour.

He behaved with great firmness.

He was then remanded to prison, and the Court proceeded to discuss their sentence, which was sent to the Lord Lieutenant for his approbation, and has not yet transpired.

BELFAST NEWS-LETTER, 13 NOVEMBER 1798

NOTHING BUT MARTIAL AUTHORITY

Phoenix Park, November 19, 1798

My dear Sir—Tone died this morning of his wound.

A writ had been moved to bring up Moore, the Rebel President of the Connaught Directory, now confined at Castlebar. It is intended that a special return should be made to the writ. The Counties of Mayo, Wicklow, and Wexford, are still so disturbed, that it is impossible, with any effect, to send the King's commission into them: nothing but martial authority can repress the daring outrages of the Rebels, who still infest those counties . . .

The despatch received from England yesterday will soon give us something to do. The opponents of the Union only wait for Government to take the first step. The Lord-Lieutenant was to see Lord Shannon this morning, and to-morrow several of the principal persons in town. We shall endeavour to have this question stated to the public in such a way, as will give a tone to our friends and literary advocates. The Bar is disposed to be very hostile . . . The question is very little understood; of course, much feared.

I have the honour to be, &c.,

CASTLEREAGH

LORD CASTLEREAGH TO MR WICKHAM, 19 NOVEMBER 1798

Whitehall, Dec. 21, 1798

MY LORD,

The King's servants are of opinion that not a moment should be lost in authorising and desiring your Excellency to state without delay to all the persons with whom you may have communications on the subject of the Union, that His Majesty's Government is determined to press that measure, as essential to the well-being of both countries, and particularly to the security and peace of Ireland, as dependent on its connection with Great Britain; that this object will now be urged to the utmost, and will even in the case, if it should happen, of any present failure, be renewed on every occasion it succeeds, and that the conduct of individuals upon this subject will be considered as the test of their disposition to support the King's Government . . .

I have, &c.,

PORTLAND

THE DUKE OF PORTLAND TO MARQUIS CORNWALLIS, 21 DECEMBER 1798

MARQUIS CORNWALLIS

1799–1801

UNION AND ANTI-UNION

Union and Anti-Union being the orders of the day here, nothing else is attended to. Every man who holds a card in the game of politics, plays to further his own views—the mass of the people are mere spectators, curious to see the result, but feeling little interest as to the particular turn it will take. The wish of every true patriot is that it may cease to be distracted by the separate views and separate interests of its parts.

THE TIMES, 9 JANUARY 1799

THE CONSOLIDATION OF THE STRENGTH OF BOTH ISLANDS

Castletown, January 15, 1799

My dear Lord—I continue still very ill with this cursed influenza, and my exertions in riding after the banditti have rather thrown me back; but give my love to Lord Cornwallis, and let him be assured that if I am able even to speak ten sentences, I will do it on Tuesday next, as nothing ever was, or is, so near my heart as the consolidation of the strength of both islands into one Legislative Union. If this can be done, in spite of the private interest of one set of men and the nonsensical noisy clamour of the other, I shall die content.

I will call on Lord Cornwallis at the Park either to-morrow or on Thursday morning, if I am able to tell him what I now tell you, being

Your affectionate Uncle and Friend,

T.C.

RIGHT HONOURABLE THOMAS CONOLLY TO LORD CASTLEREAGH, 15 JANUARY 1799

REBELLION ... NOT DEAD BUT SLEEPETH

The *Hibernian Journal*, of the 14th, says—Accounts have been received in town, that in the counties of Down, Armagh, Clare, Galway, and some others of those a short time since infested by the spirit of Rebellion—the cutting down of trees and the manufacture of pikes has recommenced with more than former avidity, in the hope that the agitation of the question of Union may revive the pretences for renovating the Rebellion, supposed to have been long since put down, but which, we are sorry to say, "Is not dead, but sleepeth."

THE TIMES, 19 JANUARY 1799

THE ASCENDANCY OF THE
PROTESTANT RELIGION

Limerick, January 20, 1799

My dear Lord—I received the honour of a very polite letter from his Excellency the Lord-Lieutenant, expressing a wish that I should attend him in Dublin as soon as I conveniently could, as the very important measure of a Union with Great Britain would be brought forward in the two Parliaments of both kingdoms at the opening of the ensuing session . . .

Your Lordship knows that I am an Englishman and a Bishop of the Church of Ireland, and therefore you cannot doubt my wishes to support any measure that may best secure the ascendancy of the Protestant religion in Ireland, and cement for ever the connexion of the two kingdoms; and I trust that you are now convinced, by my adherence to my post in the worst times of danger, that no *personal* considerations will induce me to take a lukewarm part in supporting my principles and his Majesty's Government in this country. It is my intention to hasten to Dublin as soon as my health will permit.

I have the honour to be, &c.,

THOMAS LIMERICK

THE BISHOP OF LIMERICK TO LORD CASTLEREAGH, 20 JANUARY 1799

THE ESCAPE OF DWYER

Through the activity of the Glengarry Regiment, who have in every respect conducted themselves in an exemplary manner, seven of Dwyer's gang are at present in custody at Hacketstown, and three killed.

A detachment of the above regiment, under the command of Captain

M'DONNEL and Lieutenant BETAU, in pursuance of an information, proceeded to a place called Rully-duff, and surrounded the house in which those desperadoes had assembled. Seeing no possibility of escape, the seven, now prisoners, surrendered and gave up their arms; Dwyer, however, and the three that fell, resisted, and fired several shots on the army. In consequence of this determined resistance the house was set on fire, in which they continued till its effects began to render their situation no longer bearable; the three who were killed therefore fell in their attempt to escape, having been

MICHAEL DWYER

shot as they issued from the house. Dwyer remained still–behind, but at length rushing forth amidst the flames, and favoured by the smoke, he got unperceived to some distance, and by an almost miraculous exertion of agility, affected his escape.

THE TIMES, 27 FEBRUARY 1799

AN UNFAVOURABLE TURN

DEAR ROSS,

You will have seen with sincere concern the unfavourable turn which things have taken with respect to the Union, and you will easily conceive the mischiefs which must follow.

Although all the persons who voted against that measure will not act together as a party, yet I have no doubt a formidable opposition will remain united, and that questions of tithes, emancipation, &c., &c., will be brought forward, which will tend to render Government odious to the Catholics if they are resisted, and if they should be granted, would render an Union at a future period impracticable.

The Catholics, notwithstanding their refusal to take any part as a body against the Union, still feel that their claims, even on that occasion, were to be resisted, and it is natural to suppose that they will soon be disposed to unite with those who apparently endeavour to obtain for them the immediate accomplishment of their wishes.

In the mean time we have every reason to believe that the French are meditating a serious attack, and from the most authentic channels we learn that the disaffected are more active than ever in swearing and organizing the southern provinces, to which quarter we have every reason to suppose that the next attempt will be directed . . .

God bless you. Give my kindest compliments to Mrs. Ross, and believe me, &c.,

CORNWALLIS

MARQUIS CORNWALLIS TO MAJOR-GENERAL ROSS, DUBLIN CASTLE, 28 JANUARY 1799

FRAUGHT WITH CURSES

Our unhappy distractions have been urged as a necessity for the Union. Dreadful, indeed, has been the conflict. There has been much to be lamented. There is no reason to despond. In the midst of our calamities, I discover the seeds of future aggrandizement. We have great vices. We have great virtues. Has cruelty been awake? Humanity has not slept. We have witnessed the hardy virtue of antiquity. In horror at its effects, I discern the future extinction of religious bigotry . . .

Were an extravagant young man, to secure his future frugality, to deliver his estate to the management of a *notorious old spendthrift*, and sign a bond never to call him to account for the profits? Were a freeman voluntarily to become a slave? Would you not laugh at the folly of the one, and despise the baseness of the other. Yet such will be your conduct, if you make an incorporate Union . . .

Were an Union fraught with blessings, as it is with curses—Were it the elixir of life, not the potion of death. You ought to reject it.

There are crimes which no bribe could tempt a moral man to commit.

AN ADDRESS TO THE PEOPLE OF IRELAND AGAINST A UNION, DUBLIN, 1799

MY LORD,

There is an Opposition in Parliament to the measure of Union, formidable in character and talents. Their numbers, though they have not proved equal to shake the Government, have, for the present, rendered the prosecution of the measure in Parliament impracticable. The removals in contemplation cannot fail to consolidate their party, and to render their future exertions proportionally animated ... With the concurrence and advice of the King's confidential servants, I am prepared to employ every exertion in my power to bring it to a successful issue. He must be a bold, or rather a rash, man, who would answer for either the public or parliamentary temper of this country; but after weighing the subject with all the attention I am master of I see no reason to despair of a successful issue, though the period may be delayed. After having gone so far, and the principle in question having in fact been already acted upon, I see no other alternative but to pursue the most decided line of conduct ...

CORNWALLIS

MARQUIS CORNWALLIS TO THE DUKE OF PORTLAND, DUBLIN CASTLE, 24 MAY 1799

THE MOST CORRUPT PEOPLE UNDER HEAVEN

DEAR ROSS,

Brome and Lady Louisa arrived yesterday safe and well, having been driven back to Holyhead on the 3rd, in a tremendous gale of wind ...

My occupation is now of the most unpleasant nature, negotiating and jobbing with the most corrupt people under heaven. I despise and hate myself every hour for engaging in such dirty work, and am supported only by the reflection that without an Union the British Empire must be dissolved. When it is impossible to gratify the unreasonable demands of our politicians, I often think of two lines of Swift, speaking of the Lord-Lieutenant and the system of corruption—

> "And then at Beelzebub's great hall
> Complains his budget is too small."

I am &c.,

CORNWALLIS

MARQUIS CORNWALLIS TO MAJOR-GENERAL ROSS, PHOENIX PARK, 8 JUNE 1799

EARL OF CLARE

LORD CLARE'S IMMEDIATE PROMOTION

[Secret and most Confidential.]

MY DEAR LORD,

When I received your Grace's letter suggesting the propriety of moving His Majesty to confer at this time a British peerage on Lord Clare, I was not without apprehension that it might occasion some dissatisfaction on the part of Lord Ely, whom we have at length, with much difficulty, brought to promise to take a zealous part in promoting resolutions in favour of the Union in those counties where his property gives him a considerable influence.

From a conviction, however, that it would be highly imprudent to allow Lord Ely to obtain the principal object of his wishes before that measure is carried which tends to deprive him of great portion of his importance, and from a sense of the indelicacy of suffering the Chancellor to wait for a mark of His Majesty's favour until the day of general remuneration shall arrive, I do not hesitate to give my opinion in favour of Lord Clare's immediate promotion.

I am, &c.,

CORNWALLIS

MARQUIS CORNWALLIS TO THE DUKE OF PORTLAND, DUBLIN CASTLE, 8 JULY 1799

LORD CASTLEREAGH

IN FAVOUR OF UNION

My dear Lord—Nothing could have succeeded better than Lord Cornwallis's visit to this place: all classes and descriptions of persons have been forwarded in manifesting every mark of respect and attention to his Excellency ...

Mr. May has been most strenuous and active in the arrangements in favour of Union, and has been personally attentive to Lord Cornwallis in all respects ...

I have the honour to be, &c.,

E. B. LITTLEHALES

LIEUTENANT-COLONEL LITTLEHALES TO LORD CASTLEREAGH, BELFAST, 9 OCTOBER 1799

MR. EGAN had just risen to speak, when Mr. Grattan entered the House,
supported (in consequence of illness) by Mr. W.B. Ponsonby and
Mr. Arthur Moore. He took the oaths and his seat, and after Mr. Egan had
concluded, in consequence of illness being obliged to speak sitting,
he addressed the House as follows:—

S IR, The gentleman who spoke last but one (Mr. Fox) has spoken
the pamphlet of the English minister—I answer that minister. He
has published two celebrated productions, in both of which he
declares his intolerance of the constitution of Ireland. He concurs with
the men whom he has hanged, in thinking the constitution a grievance,
and differs from them in the remedy only; they proposing to substitute
a republic, and he proposing to substitute the yoke of the British
Parliament; the one turns rebel to the King, the minister a rebel to the
constitution.

HENRY GRATTAN

We have seen him inveigh against their
projects, let us hear him in defence of his
own. He denies in the face of the two nations
a public fact registered and recorded; he dis-
claims the final adjustment of 1782, and he
tells you that this final adjustment was no
more than an incipient train of negotiation.
The settlement of which I speak consists of
several parts, every part a record, establishing
on the whole two grand positions. First, the
admission of Ireland's claim to be legislated
for by no other parliament but that of Ireland.
Secondly, the finality imposed upon the two
nations, regarding all constitutional projects
affecting each other. On the admission of that
claim, the first tracts of this adjustment are
two messages sent by his majesty to the parlia-
ments of the different countries, to come to a final adjustment, in order
to remove the discontents and jealousies of the Irish; the second, the
answer of the Parliament of Ireland to His Majesty's message, declaring,
among other causes of discontent and jealousy, one great, capital, principal, and fundamental cause, namely, the interposition of the Parliament
of Great Britain in the legislative regulation of Ireland, accompanied

with a solemn protest against that interposition, and with a claim of right on the part of Ireland; not of the Parliament of Ireland only, but of the people of the realm, whose ancient and unalienable inheritance it was stated in that address to be—a perpetual exemption against the interference of the Parliament of Great Britain, or that of any other Parliament, save only the King, Lords, and Commons of Ireland . . .

I think I have now shown, from the records quoted, that the argument of the minister is against the express letter, the evident meaning and honest sense of this final settlement, and I beg leave to repeat that finality was not only a part of the settlement, but one of its principal objects. The case is still stronger against him: finality was the principal object of his country, as legislative independency was the object of our's. Ireland wished to seize the moment of her strength for the establishment of her liberties; the court of England wished to conclude the operations of that strength, and bind its progress. The one country wished to establish her liberty, the other to check the growth of demand; I say the growth of demand; it was the expression of the time. The court of England came, therefore, to an agreement with this country, namely, to establish for ever the free and independent existence of the Irish Parliament, and to preserve for ever the unity of empire. The former, by the abovementioned adjustment, the latter, by the clause of finality to the adjustment annexed, and by precluding then, and at all times to come, the introduction of any further constitutional questions in either country, affecting the connection which was to rest under solemn covenant, inviolable, impregnable, and invincible to the intrigue or ambition of either country, founded on the prudent, the profound, the liberal, and the eternal principle of unity of empire, and separation of parliament.

I might, however, waive all this, and yet the minister would get nothing; I might allow, contrary to common sense, that final adjustment, as proposed by His Majesty, means incipient negotiation. I will suppose, contrary to truth, to public faith, public honour, and common policy, that the councils of Great Britain at that time meant to leave the Irish constitution open to the encroachments of the British Parliament, and the British empire open to the encroachments of the Irish volunteer; that is, that she meant to expose the solidity of her empire, in order to cheat the Irish, first, of their opportunity, and afterwards of their constitution; and yet he has gained nothing by these preposterous concessions, because he must allow that the arrangement did proceed to certain articles of covenant, and the first article on the part of England excludes his Union, being the assent of the Parliament of Great Britain to the requisition of the people of Ireland, which was to be exempted in all times to come from the interference of British Parliaments, and to have established over them no other legislature whatever, save only that of the King, Lords, and Commons of Ireland. Admitting, then, the ridiculous idea of ulterior measures to follow final adjustment, a Union could not be one of them. It is hardly necessary to mention that he has been minister ever since that period; that during the whole of that time he never ventured to name Union as one of those measures; not in 1783, when a bill was brought in by the ministry; not in 1785, when he introduced his celebrated propositions, and stated the second resolution of the 17th of May, 1782, to comprehend, not the constitution, but the commerce of both countries; not in the administration of 1785; not, in short, until he had reduced this country by a train of calamitous measures, to religious divisions, to the condition of a conquest, such as she was when the Parliament of England, at the close of the last century, took away her trade, and in the middle of the present took away her constitution.

HENRY GRATTAN'S SPEECH TO THE HOUSE OF COMMONS, 15 JANUARY 1800

REPRESENTATION OF A LATE UNFORTUNATE DUEL

DEAR ROSS,

After a debate of eighteen hours in the House of Commons upon an amendment proposed by the Anti-Unionists to the Address—*To maintain the independence of the Irish Parliament as settled in* 1782—the division was: For the amendment, 96; against, 138. Majority for Government, 42.

Mr. Grattan took his seat in the latter part of the debate, between 7 and 8 o'clock this morning, and made an inflammatory speech, which was most admirably answered by Corry, and G. is thought to have done more harm than good to the Opposition. I am assured that we had the advantage in speaking as well as voting; and considering the number of our friends that were out of Parliament on account of their having accepted offices, things certainly look very favourably. Lords Downshire and De Clifford were both against us: Lord Darnley is with us, but neither of his Members came over to vote.

Yours ever, &c.,

CORNWALLIS

MARQUIS CORNWALLIS TO MAJOR-GENERAL ROSS, DUBLIN CASTLE, 16 JANUARY 1800

THE UNION IS CARRIED

DEAR ROSS,

After a debate of twenty hours we carried the first proposition in the committee—"That a legislative Union of the two kingdoms was desirable," by a majority of 46. There was no appearance of defection amongst our supporters, so that I trust the measures will be carried.

Corry very unwisely made another attack on Grattan, who had rather the advantage afterwards in his replies, with respect to abuse, and then wounded him (Corry) in the arm, in a meeting in the Phoenix Park. This is unlucky, and tends rather to raise Grattan, who was as low before as his enemies could wish. I write in great haste.

Most truly yours,

CORNWALLIS

MARQUIS CORNWALLIS TO MAJOR-GENERAL ROSS, DUBLIN CASTLE, 18 FEBRUARY 1800

Whereas in pursuance of his Majesty's most gracious recommendation to the two houses of parliament in Great Britain and Ireland respectively, to consider of such measures as might best tend to strengthen and consolidate the connexion between the two kingdoms, the two houses of the parliament of Great Britain, and the two houses of the parliament of Ireland have severally agreed and resolved, that in order to promote and secure the essential interests of Great Britain and Ireland, and to consolidate the strength, power, and resources of the British empire, it will be advisable to concur in such measures as may best tend to unite the two kingdoms of Great Britain and Ireland, into one kingdom, in such manner, and on such terms and conditions, as may be established by the acts of the respective parliaments of Great Britain and Ireland.

And whereas in furtherance of the said resolution, both houses of the said two parliaments respectively have likewise agreed upon certain articles for effectuating and establishing the said purposes in the tenor following:

ARTICLE FIRST

That it be the first article of the union of the kingdoms of Great Britain and Ireland, that the said kingdoms of Great Britain and Ireland shall, upon the first day of January, which shall be in the year of our lord one thousand eight hundred and one, and for ever, be united into one kingdom, by the name of "the united kingdom of Great Britain and Ireland," and that the royal stile and titles appertaining to the imperial crown of the said united kingdom and its dependencies, and also the ensigns, armorial flags and banners thereof, shall be such as his Majesty by his royal proclamation under the great seal of the united kingdom shall be pleased to appoint.

ARTICLE SECOND

That it be the second article of union, that the succession to the imperial crown of the said united kingdom, and of the dominions thereunto belonging, shall continue limited and settled in the same manner as the succession to the imperial crown of the said kingdoms of Great Britain and Ireland now stands limited and settled, according to the existing laws, and to the terms of union between England and Scotland.

ARTICLE THIRD

That it be the third article of union, that the said united kingdom be represented in one and the same parliament, to be stiled "The parliament of the united kingdom of Great Britain and Ireland."

ARTICLE FOURTH

That it be the fourth article of union that four lords spiritual of Ireland, by rotation of sessions, and twenty-eight lords temporal of Ireland, elected for life by the peers of Ireland, shall be the number to sit and vote on the part of Ireland in the house of lords of the parliament of the united kingdom, and one hundred commoners, (two for each county of Ireland, two for the city of Dublin, two for the city of Cork, one for the university of Trinity college, and one for each of the thirty-one most considerable cities, towns, and boroughs) be the number to sit and vote on the part of Ireland in the house of commons of the parliament of the united kingdom . . .

ARTICLE FIFTH

That it be the fifth article of union, that the churches of England and Ireland, as now by law established, be united into one protestant episcopal church, to be called, "The united church of England and Ireland," and that the doctrine, worship, discipline and government of the said united church shall be, and shall remain in full force for ever, as the same are now by law established for the church of England . . .

ARTICLE SIXTH

That it be the sixth article of union, that his Majesty's subjects of Great Britain and Ireland shall, from and after the fifth day of January, one thousand eight hundred and one, be entitled to the same privileges, and be on the same footing as to encouragements and bounties . . .

ARTICLE SEVENTH

That it be the seventh article of union that the charge arising from the payment of the interest and the sinking fund for the reduction of principal of the debt incurred in either kingdom before the union shall continue to be separately defrayed by Great Britain and Ireland respectively, except as hereinafter provided.

ARTICLE EIGHTH

That it be the eighth article of union, that all laws in force at the time of the union, and all the courts of civil and ecclesiastical jurisdiction within the respective kingdoms, shall remain as now by law established within the same, subject only to such alterations and regulations from time to time as circumstances may appear to the parliament of the united kingdom to require ... present in force in either kingdom, which shall be contrary to any of the provisions which may be enacted by any act for carrying these articles into effect, be from and after the union repealed.

And whereas the said articles having by address of the respective houses of parliament in Great Britain and Ireland been humbly laid before his Majesty, his Majesty has been graciously pleased to approve the same, and to recommend it to his two houses of parliament in Great Britain and Ireland, to consider of such measures as may be necessary for giving effect to the said articles: In order therefore to give full effect and validity to the same, be it enacted by the King's most excellent Majesty, by and with the advice and consent of the lords spiritual and temporal, and commons in this present parliament assembled, and by the authority of the same, That the said foregoing recited articles, each and every one of them, according to the true intent and tenor thereof, be ratified, confirmed and approved, and be, and they are hereby declared to be, the articles of the union of Great Britain and Ireland, and the same shall be in force and have effect for ever, from the first day of January, which shall be in the year of our Lord, one thousand eight hundred and one.

AN ACT FOR THE UNION OF GREAT BRITAIN AND IRELAND,

FRIDAY THE FIRST DAY OF AUGUST, ONE THOUSAND EIGHT HUNDRED,

ROYAL ASSENT GIVEN

1801–1803

PARLIAMENT MEETS

This being the day appointed for the Meeting of the Imperial Parliament, the same was opened by Commission, and the Commons being sent for to the House of Peers, the Lord Chancellor signified, that it was his majesty's pleasure to defer declaring the causes of his assembling the parliament, until the Commons had chosen a Speaker.

MR. ADDINGTON CHOSEN SPEAKER.

Mr. *Addington* was then conducted to the Chair. He said he had to intreat the House to accept his most grateful acknowledgments for the high honour they had done him in placing him in the Chair, and above all for the manner in which that honour had been conferred. He begged leave to assure them it had made a deep and lasting impression on his mind.

Lord *Hawkesbury* congratulated the right hon. gentleman on his situation ... He concluded by moving to adjournment; which was agreed to.

On the following day, Mr. Addington was presented to the Lords Commissioners and approved of.

THE KINGS'S SPEECH ON OPENING THE SESSION.

February 2. His Majesty went in state to the House of Peers, and opened the session with the following Speech to both Houses:

"My Lords, and Gentlemen;

"At a crisis so important to the interests of my people, I derive great satisfaction from being enabled, for the first time, to avail myself of the advise and assistance of the parliament of my united kingdom of Great Britain and Ireland.

"This memorable aera, distinguished by the accomplishment of a measure calculated to augment and consolidate the strength and resources of the empire, and to cement more closely the interests and affections of my subjects, will, I trust, be equally marked by that vigour, energy, and firmness, which the circumstances of our present situation peculiarly require.

"The unfortunate course of events on the continent, and the consequences which must be expected to result from it, cannot fail to be matter of anxiety and concern to all who have a just feeling for the security and independence of Europe.

"Your astonishment, as well as your regret, must be excited by the conduct of those powers whose attention, at such a period, appears to be more engaged in endeavours to weaken the naval force of the British empire, which has hitherto opposed so powerful an obstacle to the inordinate ambition of France, than in concerting the means of mutual defence against their common and increasing danger.

"The Representations which I directed to be made to the court of Petersburgh, in consequence of the outrages committed against the ships, property, and persons, of my subjects, have been treated with the utmost disrespect; and the proceedings of which I complained have been aggravated by subsequent acts of injustice and violence.

"Under these circumstances a Convention has been concluded by that court with those of Copenhagen and Stockholm, the object of which, as avowed by one of the contracting parties, is, to renew their former engagements for establishing, by force, a new code of maritime law, inconsistent with the rights, and hostile to the interests of this country.

"In this situation, I could not hesitate as to the conduct which it became me to pursue. I have taken the earliest measures to repel the aggressions of this hostile confederacy, and to support those principles which are essential to the maintenance of our naval strength, and which are grounded on the system of public law, so long established and recognized in Europe.

"I have, at the same time, given such assurances, as manifest my disposition to renew my ancient relations with those powers, whenever it can be done consistently with the honour of my crown, and with a just regard to the safety of my subjects. You will, I am persuaded, omit nothing on your part, that can afford me the most vigorous and effectual support in my firm determination to maintain to the utmost, against every attack, the naval rights and the interests of my empire.

"Gentlemen of the House of Commons;

"I have directed the estimates for the several branches of the public service to be laid before you: deeply as I lament the continued necessity of adding to the burthens of my people, I am persuaded you will feel with me the importance of providing effectual means for those exertions which are indispensably requisite for the honour and security of the country.

"My Lords and Gentlemen;

"I am confident that your deliberations will be uniformly directed to the great object of improving the benefits of that happy Union, which, by the blessing of Providence, has now been effected; and of promoting, to the utmost, the prosperity of every part of my dominions.

"You will, I doubt not, resume the enquiries which were so diligently prosecuted in the last session of parliament, as to the best means of relieving my subjects from the pressure of the present high price of provisions; and of preventing, as far as it can be done by human foresight, the recurrence of similar difficulties. In these endeavours, and in every measure that can contribute to the happiness of my people, the great end of all my wishes, you may be assured of my cordial concurrence.

"You may rely on my availing myself of the earliest opportunity which shall afford a prospect of terminating the present contest, on grounds consistent with our security and honour, and with the maintenance of those essential rights on which our naval strength must always principally depend.

"It will afford me the truest and most heartfelt satisfaction whenever the disposition of our enemies shall enable me thus to restore to the subjects of my united kingdom the blessings of peace, and thereby confirm and augment those advantages which result from our internal situation, and which, even under all the difficulties of war, have carried to so great an extent the agriculture, manufactures, commerce, and revenue of the country."

FIRST SESSION OF THE FIRST PARLIAMENT OF THE UNITED KINGDOM OF GREAT BRITAIN
AND IRELAND, 22 JANUARY 1801

NO CATHOLIC EMANCIPATION

SIR, I cannot but regret that on the late unhappy occasion I had not been treated with more confidence previous to forming an opinion, which, to my greatest surprise, I learnt on Thursday from Earl Spencer has been in agitation ever since Lord Castlereagh came over in August, yet of which I never had the smallest suspicion till within these very few weeks; but so desirous was I to avoid the present conclusion, that, except what passed with Earl Spencer and Lord Grenville about three weeks past, and a hint I gave to Mr. Secretary Dundas on Wednesday sevenight, I have been silent on the subject, and, indeed, hoping that Mr. Pitt had not pledged himself on what I cannot with my sentiments of religious and political duty think myself at liberty to concur. Mr. Secretary Dundas has

MR DUNDAS

known my opinions when he corresponded with the Earl of Westmorland, then Lord-Lieutenant of Ireland, and at least will do me the justice to recollect that both then, and when afterwards brought forward by the Earl Fitzwilliam, my language perfectly coincided with my present conduct.

GEORGE R.

KING GEORGE III TO THE RIGHT HONOURABLE HENRY DUNDAS, WINDSOR, 7 FEBRUARY 1801

TO TRANQUILLIZE THE MINDS OF
THE CATHOLICS

DEAR ROSS,

No consideration could induce me to take a responsible part with any Administration who can be so blind to the interest, and indeed to the immediate security of their country, as to persevere in the old system of proscription and exclusion in Ireland. My sentiments on this head are sufficiently known, and I have heard from pretty good authority that my successor is fixed ... I feel it, however, to be my duty to my country, not to quit my station angrily, and to employ such reasonable space of time as it may suit Government to take in sending over a successor, in endeavouring to tranquillize the minds of the Catholics, to persuade them to wait with patience for the accomplishment of their wishes, which, although it is not so near as we had reason to expect, may nevertheless, from the eminent characters of all parties who are pledged in their favour, still be considered as ultimately secure, and by every means in my power to prevent such immediate effects of their disappointment, as would, under our present difficulties, tend to the utter destruction of the empire ...

I am, &c.,

CORNWALLIS

MARQUIS CORNWALLIS TO MAJOR-GENERAL ROSS, DUBLIN CASTLE, 15 FEBRUARY 1801

JULY.— We arrived in Ireland on the 20th July, 1801, and stayed there till 30th January, 1802.

Of these six months, the two first were a time of war, and daily expectation of rebellion and invasion.

During this period the chief business of the Irish Government was to revise the proceedings and sentences of all courts martial for the execution of the Martial Law Act, and to correspond with the generals of districts upon the civil and military state of the country. Upon the news of the French preparations in the Channel, the Irish Government obtained the offers of all the Irish militia regiments to volunteer for service in England, if it should be attacked. Proclamations were also issued for regulating the mode of driving cattle in all the maritime counties, and the secret orders were renewed to each general, directing his line of conduct, according to the plans laid down by Lord Cornwallis.

CHARLES ABBOT

The regular forces in Ireland, including fencibles during this period, was about 30,000, and the militia 30,000 more: the yeomanry corps of infantry and cavalry were about 60,000; the cavalry part being about 12,000.

Lord Cornwallis's plan for the defence of Ireland led him to reduce the Artillery to a very small force. He withdrew almost all the heavy guns from all the fortresses on the coast; and proposed to employ very little of even Horse Artillery in the field; and Lieutenant-General Floyd concurred with other officers who spoke with me upon the subject in thinking it much too small.

The principal outrages during this time were committed in the county of Limerick, though they were frequent also in other parts; and lights at night upon the mountains of Wicklow and Wexford, and the reappearance of the disaffected in Dublin, excited considerable alarms.

During the month of August I made a short tour with the Lord-Lieutenant to the Military Road, in the county of Wicklow, to the

Gold Mines of Croaghan, and to Arklow, where we saw the field of battle between the rebels and General Needham, in which Father Murphy was killed. We went also to view the Harbour of Wicklow. In consequence of this tour a large extension of the Military Road was resolved upon, and special reports were ordered to be made upon a more effectual plan for working the Gold Mine, and also for improving the Harbour of Wicklow.

DIARY OF CHARLES ABBOT, LORD COLCHESTER, JULY 1801–JANUARY 1802

A CHANCE ENCOUNTER

22 Ventose—Hotel de Rome, Rue St. Dominique, Fauxbourgs St. Germain

EARL MOUNT CASHEL

A Month has passed since I last wrote ... We have lately become acquainted with Robert Emmett, who I dare say you have heard of, as being amongst the politically distinguish'd in Dublin College. His face is uncommonly expressive of everything youthful, and everything enthusiastic, and his colour comes and goes so rapidly, accompanied by such a nervousness of agitated sensibility, that in his society I feel in a perpetual apprehension lest any passing idle word shou'd wound the delicacy of his feelings. For tho' his reserve prevents one's hearing many of his opinions, yet one would swear to their style of exaltation, from their flitting shadows blushing across his countenance in everlasting succession. His understanding they tell me is very bright. But I am not likely to know much about it. For his extreme prejudice against French society will prevent our meeting him anywhere except at the House of an English gentleman, who is soon returning to London. At this house we have seen the widow of the unfortunate Tone, who is interesting to the greatest degree.

DIARY OF EARL MOUNT CASHEL, 13 MARCH 1802

The King's Message relative to the Termination of the Discussions with France. May 16. The Chancellor of the Exchequer presented the following Message from his Majesty:

"G. R.

"His majesty thinks it proper to acquaint the House of Commons, that the discussions which he announced to them, in his Message of the 8th of March last, as then subsisting between his majesty and the French government, have been terminated; that the conduct of the French government has obliged his majesty to recall his ambassador from Paris, and that the ambassador from the French republic has left London.

"His majesty has given directions for laying before the House of Commons, with as little delay as possible, copies of such Papers as will afford the fullest information to his parliament at this important conjuncture.

"It is a consolation to his majesty to reflect, that no endeavours have been wanting on his part to preserve to his subjects the blessings of peace; but under the circumstances which have occurred to disappoint his just expectations, his majesty relies with confidence on the zeal and public spirit of his faithful Commons, and on the exertions of his brave and loyal subjects to support him in his determination to employ the power and resources of the nation, in opposing the spirit of ambition and encroachment which at present actuates the councils of France, in upholding the dignity of his crown, and in asserting and maintaining the rights and interests of his people.   G. R."

HANSARD'S PARLIAMENTARY DEBATES, 16 MAY 1803

INFLAMMABLE MATERIALS

Private and Confidential

My dear Lord Castlereagh ... As your Lordship is no doubt thoroughly informed of the situation of affairs in this country, I have no great occasion to trouble you with any observations on the subject, but to say that we still continue to enjoy internal tranquillity.

The disposition in the North is unquestionably at this moment more

194 cordial to Government, from all that I can collect, than it has been for years past. Without entering into particulars, it is understood that the Northern Sectarists hold a language very inimical to the views and conduct of Buonaparte, and consider his despotic intentions of aggrandizement utterly subversive of every principle of civil liberty; and, from all accounts, the northern people do not hesitate loudly to exclaim against him for his oppression and tyrannical behaviour towards the Swiss.

Your Lordship, however, is too well acquainted with the inflammable materials of which Ireland is composed, to appreciate too highly or over-estimate the present comfortable posture of things, in comparison to what they have been, or may be, if we are again to be menaced with invasion from our implacable enemy . . .

E.B. LITTLEHALES

LIEUTENANT-COLONEL LITTLEHALES TO LORD CASTLEREAGH, DUBLIN CASTLE, 25 MAY 1803

'LOVE THE BROTHERHOOD, FEAR GOD AND HONOUR THE KING'

As it redounds much to the credit of the Orangemen of Ireland, that they stood forward in the hour of danger, to defend the religion, the laws, and constitution of their country; so the Masters of the several Orange Societies in the county of Antrim, assembled at their annual meeting in Lisburn, on the 6th day of June, 1803, think it proper to address their brethren at this juncture, when war is renewed with their ancient and inveterate enemy, whose views of ambition and aggrandizement have disdained to be confined within due bounds. They call upon and urge them, by every tie which binds them to the discharge, of the most important duties, that they will continue to exert all their powers to guard and defend those invaluable interests, which are the objects of their association. They congratulate their brethren and their countrymen in general, on entering into the present contest with more favourable prospects, than any period of the late war presented. They have reason to believe, that the number of internal enemies is greatly diminished; that the folly and madness of attempting to overturn our happy constitution, established under the auspices of our great deliverer, William, Prince of Orange, is more evident; and that no man who is not a decided traitor to his country, will now be disposed to sacrifice those inestimable advantages, which have been matured and confirmed by the wisdom of ages, for such speculative doctrines and idle theories, as have been demonstrated, when reduced to practice, to lead only to anarchy, slavery, and arbitrary power. Strange however as it may seem, there is still cause to fear that some such traitors do exist; and therefore Orangemen are called upon to be on their guard against them; to be ever ready, like watchful centinels, at their posts, to defend the constitution against the first attempts of all its foes. By so doing, they will hand down to posterity the character of intrepid and unshaken loyalty, which they have justly acquired; and of having materially contributed to the safety and protection of their country.

Let us ever keep in mind the true spirit of our institution; that we entertain no enmity to any man, whatever may be his religious persuasion, who is not an enemy to the state; and that we consider every good subject as a friend and co-adjutor with us in the glorious and patriotic cause, which animates our exertions. Let us "love the Brotherhood, fear God, and honour the King."

(SIGNED BY ORDER,)

WILLIAM HART, G. SEC. COUNTY ANTRIM.

AN ADDRESS OF THE MASTERS OF THE SEVERAL ORANGE SOCIETIES IN THE COUNTY OF ANTRIM, 6 JUNE 1803, ON A RENEWAL OF THE WAR WITH FRANCE, BELFAST, 1803

GENERAL STATEMENT OF THE MATTERS RELATING TO THE INSURRECTION OF 23 JULY 1803

The investigation of the circumstances attending the Insurrection which lately took place in Dublin has led to a full disclosure of the original design of the parties engaged, and the principal facts which occurred on that occasion. From the nature of the attempt which was made, great uncertainty existed as to the extent of the danger, and that much misapprehension, and even misrepresentation, took place, was almost a natural consequence.

It is now known that the design of the attempt, which was afterwards made in July last, was conceived in France about the middle of the last winter. Previous to that period, the probability of a war with England had made the Government of France turn their thoughts to an expedition to Ireland . . .

ROBERT EMMET

Encouraged, no doubt, by the French Government (who, as well as some of his associates, were probably unacquainted with the whole of his object) the sanguine disposition of the younger Emmett, who was last winter in Paris, led him to conceive a plan for effecting a Revolution in Ireland, separating it from England, and establishing an independent power in this country, capable of foreign relations, before the French should have their plans matured for an invasion and a conquest.

With this view, there is reason to think that he communicated with several of the exiled Irish then in France, and particularly with his brother T.A. Emmett, and Macnevin . . .

Many exiled Irish were then on the continent; but it appears that Mr. Emmett did not succeed in getting more than Russel and Quigley to engage in the expedition to Ireland. Russel was one of the prisoners who had been confined at Fort George, and, although not a principal in the Rebellion of 1798, was of consequence enough at that time to be selected as one of the most dangerous, whom it was necessary to confine until the end of the war. He was a man of a particular and an enthusiastic turn of mind: connected with several persons in the North of Ireland by an early political alliance, and with some of them by a religious folly, he persuaded himself that he had influence enough to raise the Province of Ulster, or even a greater district.

Quigley was a man of mean condition, a bricklayer by trade, who had been confined with the State prisoners at Kilmainham gaol, and remained there until the end of the war . . .

Russel engaged his nephew, a Mr. Hamilton, a man who, it now appears, had served in the French armies, to join him, and measures were settled for the journey of the whole party to Ireland. Emmett and Russel reached Dublin early in the year. Hamilton gave Quigley and two others, his companions from Kilmainham, ten guineas each, to bear their expenses to Ireland . . .

On their arrival in Dublin, they met Emmett, and the three together consulted on their future operations . . .

The report of Russel's return attracted attention; and Quigley's having gone into the County of Kildare soon made his arrival public . . .

Reports were circulated that rebels of 1798, of much greater consequence than those mentioned, had returned to the country. The elder Emmett, O'Connor, Macnevin, Lawless, and others, it was asserted, were here; it now appears that none of them were, and, had they been concerned, additional means would have existed of discovering the conspiracy which was then concerting, and which received its chief protection from the insignificancy of the parties engaged in it . . .

Mr. Emmett . . . conceived the design of providing arms for those whose assistance he relied upon; and, full of the opinion that the disposition to revolt was as strong amongst the lower orders of the people as in his own mind, he relied upon it that the whole would be effected, if he could secure a magazine from which, on a sudden, the mob might be armed. The scene of this exploit was fixed in Dublin; and, although he held communication with parts of Ireland more distant, it does not appear that they were organized, or that he had made connections with more than a very few of the Rebels of 1798.

Having a mind much turned to military affairs, and being a student in chemistry, he prepared a system of tactics, and at the same time constructed machines, (certainly complex and ill adapted) in which gunpowder was wrought into its most pernicious forms; but he seems to have neglected the more obvious and certain modes of giving force to an effort which could alone be made by the rudest and most inexpert hands.

For the purpose of forming this magazine, a warehouse was taken in a yard, in an obscure lane, in a populous but unobserved quarter of the city. A carpenter in Emmett's confidence was the ostensible proprietor; and in this yard and warehouse were prepared the pikes and ammunition which were afterwards to be delivered to the mob . . .

Soon after Lord Whitworth's return, in May, it was perceived that some cabal had commenced among men who were before suspected, and whose conduct soon attracted a stricter observation. One of this party held a direct communication with Government, and meetings and conversations were often reported, but they led to nothing material; no organization nor system was attempted; no persons who could be seized and detained by law could be discovered, and nothing but general expression of hopes, and an increased rumour of danger, could be learned. At the same time, the reports from the country, with the exception of Kildare, (and even from thence they were not bad) were of the most favourable kind; and, as far as it was possible to reason upon the apparent dispositions of the people, a revolt could not be considered as immediate, unless in the event of a successful attempt at invasion by the enemy.

It is manifest, however, that Emmett staked his whole game on the depôt ...

In the interval between March and July, there is scarcely a trace of any correspondence with France, or any thing to show that France was much concerned in what was going on here.

Much was asserted as to the existence of such an intercourse in the months of June and July; but the proofs of it are inconsiderable ...

In the counties of Ireland, with the exception of Kildare and Wicklow, it now appears that very few had been gained over by the Conspirators. In the North, it is evident that but little preparation was made. Russel distrusted many of his old friends, and did not apply to them. He soon discovered that, among the Protestants of the North, his plans met no encouragement; which made him resort to the Defenders, or Catholics, and his very limited success with them has been sufficiently exposed ...

To aid the attack in Dublin, it now appears that only Kildare, Wicklow, and Wexford were relied upon ...

As Mr. Emmett's object was to effect a Revolution in Ireland, and to get possession of the country before the French should attempt an invasion, it was necessary for him to bring his projects speedily into action. An accident that happened in Patrick Street, which was a sort of workshop to the depôt, did, however, accelerate the execution of his design. In a room, where some combustible matter was preparing, a small quantity of gunpowder took fire, and the explosion attracted the attention of the neighbourhood. Of three men, who were in the room, two were considerably burnt, and one of them, in running his naked arm through a pane of glass, to let in air to prevent suffocation, cut himself so much the he bled to death. The cause of the explosion was not immediately understood: the neighbours were refused admittance to the house, and, before an officer of police was found to attend, ammunition and some machines were conveyed out of it. Of the former, a cask was stopped in the street by the watch, and rescued from them; every means was used to trace a connection between that house and the persons who were suspected, but without success ...

In the week which followed this explosion, Emmett determined to attempt an insurrection . . .

Although it appeared that in the country a knowledge of what was intended had spread, and that several persons at the end of the week had come into town, there was no account of any bodies of people, armed or tumultuous, having anywhere assembled; and could it be imagined that, with a garrison of three thousand men, the seat of Government, protected by seven hundred men, either within side the Castle, or within two hundred yards of it, a tumultuary attempt could excite dismay, or a doubt of its speedy suppression? . . .

Emmett was by no means satisfied that his preparations were sufficiently advanced: he had spent all his money, and had not got a fresh supply; he was not confident as to the number of his men, and he wanted further time to complete his complicated machines. It was, however, too late to recede, and he decided upon a prompt effort against the opinion of some of his associates.

At nine o'clock, as near as it can be ascertained, Emmett and his associates sallied forth from the depôt in Mass Lane. Pikes were delivered out in large quantities from this secret magazine, but they wanted men and order, and a plan which was practicable with such raw troops and rude implements. Emmett and his party paraded with their swords drawn, and firing pistols into Thomas Street. He could count but eighty followers at the time he left the depôt, and, when he reached the Market House in Thomas Street, nearly the whole had deserted him, except about twenty. Upon seeing himself thus abandoned, he quitted the street, and, with ten or twelve of his lieutenant-generals and colonels as he fancied to call them, (himself and some others being in green uniforms) he proceeded by Francis Street out of the town, and to the mountains.

The rabble whom he left behind, deserted by their leaders, armed themselves with pikes, and some two or three who remained among them assumed a command, and endeavoured to lead them to the attack of the Castle, from whence they were more than half a mile distant. That they did not obey was, perhaps, more from violence than choice, and, in an endeavour to rally them, they were carried back nearly to the spot from whence they first proceeded with arms. Here they met the carriage of the ever to be lamented Lord Kilwarden; others, who continued in the lane from whence the pikes were delivered, massacred the unfortunate Colonel Browne; and other murders were committed before the casual arrival of the party from Cork Street Barracks, by the fire of which they were routed from this disgraceful scene . . .

Notwithstanding that the rein of disaffection was let loose, and the loyal subject for a while dismayed, it is consolatory to find that in so very inconsiderable a degree was the first burst of rebellion followed in other places, or by a continuance of outrage. What took place had the most terrifying and dismaying concomitants—weapons, ammunition, murders. What would be the last act of another conspiracy was the first of this; but, while much is due to the loyal and patriotic for the fortunate results of this most mischievous attempt, let us also entertain hopes that much is also due to the ameliorated disposition of our countrymen, who were formerly deceived from their allegiance, from their interests, from their religion and their happiness, by the more systematic and not less mischievous partisans of Revolution.

DIARY OF LORD CASTLEREAGH, JULY 1803

THE TRIAL OF EMMET

Monday, September 19th, 1803

The Court sat pursuant to Adjournment
Judges present:— Lord NORBURY, Mr. *Baron* GEORGE,
and Mr. *Baron* DALY
Robert Emmet, Esq. was put upon his trial
Lord NORBURY

Gentlemen of the Jury,

I shall not delay you longer, than I feel my indispensable duty requires. We have all a very serious duty to perform. I shall not consume a moment of your time by recapitulating any principles of law, for no difficulty exists in the case, in that respect. If there had been an opportunity to make a defence in matter of law, there are no more able men for the purpose, than those who have been assigned as counsel to the prisoner; but they have comported themselves with a discretion and a manliness that is deserving of respect.

Gentlemen, it is necessary that you should know what the overt acts are to which the evidence is applicable. The Indictment is for *High Treason*, comprehending three-several branches of the statute of *Edward* the third.—First for compassing and imagining the death of the King.—Secondly.—For adhering to the King's enemies—and Thirdly—for compassing to levy war. The first overt act in support of these charges, is that the Prisoner did with others meet, consult, conspire and agree to raise, levy and make cruel insurrection, rebellion and war against the King, and to procure great quantities of arms and ammunition for the purpose of the said rebellion, and to overturn the constitution. The second is, that he did procure great quantities of arms and ammunition, and did procure to be made 1000 pikes, with intent that divers traitors should be armed therewith, and should use the same in and for making and carrying on insurrection, rebellion and war against the King, and for committing a cruel slaughter against his subjects. The third is, that he did become one of a society of persons, associated under the name of *The Provisional Government*, for the purpose of levying war against the King, and overturning the constitution, he well knowing the purposes for which that society was formed. The fourth is, that he did compose and write a certain manifesto, purporting to be a proclamation of *The Provisional Government*, and purporting that they had determined to separate *Ireland* from *England*, and for that purpose to make war against the King and his troops, with intent that said proclamation should be spread among the people, to unite them to war against the King. The fifth is, that he did write that proclamation, describing it to be the proclamation of persons unknown associated under the name of the *Provisional Government*, with the same intent as in the former. The sixth is, that he kept and concealed the Proclamation with intent that it should be published and spread amongst the people—and the seventh is, that he did ordain, prepare, levy, and make public war against the King. The same overt acts are stated in support of the second count, and there is one in support of the third, that he did with other persons actually levy war against the King.

Gentlemen, having now disposed of that which is the legal import of the charge, I shall proceed to the evidence.

ROBERT EMMET

(Here his Lordship minutely stated from his notes all the evidence which had been adduced, and accompanied this detail with occasional observations.)

As has been observed on, if the witness appears to have been an accomplice in the crimes of the prisoner, he said, it has been long settled law, that an accomplice is a competent witness to be received to give evidence, otherwise many dangerous crimes would go unpunished, and undiscovered.—But the Jury are to determine under all the circumstances appearing in the case, what credit he deserves, and where he tells a natural and consistent story. In the present instance, the witness appears consistent, and is corroborated in many particulars, and he is not contradicted in any.

(After stating and observing upon the written evidence, his Lordship proceeded.)

Now, Gentlemen, I have to conclude this duty of addressing you with one or two observations—Probably you have made a clear arrangement of this case in your own minds. But it appears to me, that there are three distinct periods, into which the facts of the case may be divided.—First, that which relates to the conduct of the Prisoner before the rebellion—Second, that which relates to his conduct on the 23rd of *July*, when the rebellion was raging, and thirdly, that which relates to his conduct afterwards—then you will consider upon the whole of the facts whether they all correspond and tend to support the general mass of charge, or whether you can form a just conclusion. It remains uncontroverted—that the prisoner had been abroad lately, and that he returned to this country, and then appeared openly. But it has been proved that in the month of *April*, upon the breaking out of the war, he disguises his name and character, and from that time until he is taken, he never goes by his own genuine name. He lives in a sequestered way—he conceals his name, and assumes that by which he was afterwards known in the *depot*—he lives there for a week before the rebellion broke out, and as to his conduct there, many facts have been proved by the witnesses, who are not contradicted. He has been proved by three witnesses to have acted there as the first in command, and to have had there that uniform in which he appeared at other places subsequent to the rebellion, and which was described to you by the farmer, and of which he spoke to his own friend Mr. *Palmer* of *Harold's-cross*, who also proved his lamenting the loss of the *depot*.

Now, then, as to the third period, what happened after the 23rd of *July*? the prisoner went to the country dressed in that same uniform.—He proceeded to the neighbourhood of *Tallagh*, in company with two others in rebel uniforms, *Doyle* indentifies the Prisoner in the situation beyond controversy, and Mrs. *Bagenal* strongly corroborates. The Prisoner at the bar, during these periods passed under different names; he was *Ellis*, he was *Hewitt*, he was *Cunningham*, and at last when made a captive, but not till then, he acknowledged his name to be *Emmet*,—He took particular pains to disguise himself at *Harold's-cross*,—he refused to have his name put on the door—he endeavoured to escape, was secured by Major *Sirr*, and is now brought to the bar—and I am sure, if I could with just propriety express my concern at seeing such a young gentleman at this bar, I would readily do so, but if you gentlemen shall be of opinion that the accusation against him is well founded, it is well for the community that he is there. It was my duty to condense the evidence into as narrow a compass as I could, and I have been obliged to state the facts which have been proved by the parol and written evidence, accompanying them with observations, which are submitted entirely to you, for you are to determine upon them all—and upon the credit of those who proved them.

Gentlemen, no witnesses have been called for the Prisoner at that bar, and now you have your duty to perform.—If you have a rational doubt—such as rational men may entertain upon the evidence, whether the Prisoner was engaged in these transactions, you should acquit him;—If you believe the evidence, it is direct proof of all the treasons charged against him.—But I say, if you have a doubt, you should acquit him.—If you do not entertain any doubt, but that you believe the evidence and the criminal conduct and intentions imputed to the Prisoner, you are bound to decide between the Prisoner and the justice due to your country, and in that case you should find him guilty.

The jury did not retire from the box, and after a few minutes deliberation, the foreman addressed the court:—

FOREMAN—My Lord, I have consulted my brother jurors, and we are all of opinion, that the Prisoner is *Guilty*.

Mr. ATTORNEY GENERAL. My Lord, it remains for me to pray the judgment of the court upon the Prisoner.

Clerk of the Crown. Gaoler, put Robert *Emmett*, Esq. to the bar.

Mr. MACNALLY. My Lords, I hope I am not intruding upon the court, and that it is not incompatible with my duty, now that the verdict has been pronounced, to state a request of the Prisoner which probably ought to be addressed to the ATTORNEY GENERAL, rather than to the court—it is, that the motion for judgment might not be made until to-morrow.

Mr. ATTORNEY GENERAL. My Lord, I have made the motion, and it is impossible for me now to comply with the request.

The *Clerk of the Crown* read the indictment and stated the verdict found in the usual form.—He then concluded thus:—"What have you therefore now to say, why judgement of death and execution should not be awarded against you according to law?"

REPORT OF THE TRIAL OF ROBERT EMMET UPON AN INDICTMENT FOR HIGH TREASON
DUBLIN, 1803

EMMET'S SPEECH FROM THE DOCK

L ord *Norbury* having ably charged the jury, recapitulated the evidence to them, and observed upon such points as needed legal illustration, they without quitting the box returned a verdict, Guilty.

The prisoner having been asked by the Clerk of the Crown what he had to say, why judgement of death and execution thereupon should not be awarded against him, said that why the judgement of the law should not pass upon him he had nothing to say; but why his character should not be relieved from the imputations thrown out against it he had much to say. He did not imagine the Court would give credit to what he was going to utter; he had no hopes that he could anchor his character to the breast of the Court; he only wished they might allow it to float down their memories till it found some more hospitable harbour to shelter it from the flames with which it was at present buffeted. He then proceeded to state the motives on which he had acted in furtherance of the insurrection of the 23rd of *July*, in which he stated that he was not the head and life's blood of that insurrection: when he came to *Ireland* he found the business ripe;—he was asked to join in it:—he took time to consider, and after mature deliberation he became one of the Provisional Government. He also further informed the Court that there was, and still is, an agent from the United Irishmen and Provisional Government of *Ireland* at *Paris* negotiating with the *French* government to obtain from them an aid sufficient to accomplish the separation of *Ireland* from *England*, the preliminary to which assistance was a guarantee to *Ireland*, similar to that which *Franklin* obtained for *America*. As to the insinuation that he intended to sell *Ireland* to *France*, it was false. God forbid he should ever see that country have any dominion or authority in *Ireland*, and he hoped that his country, if a hostile attempt of that kind was made, would meet them on the strands with a torch in one hand and the sword in the other. That if they were forced to retire before superior discipline they would burn up every blade of grass in their retreat; and if they were forced to the centre of the country, they would collect their property, and their wives and daughters and form a circle around them, and when they had fought until only two remained, the last of those two men should set fire to the pile and free them from *French* tyranny. He then proceeded to deprecate the conduct of the *French* towards those countries to which they had promised liberty and afterwards inflamed. He instanced the conduct of that nation towards *Switzerland*, where it was stated he had been; yet had the people there been desirous for *French* assistance, he would have sided with the people, he would have stood between them and the *French* whose aid they called in, and to the utmost of his ability have protected them from every attempt at subjugation, he would have done the same with the people of *Ireland*, if he could be called on to do it again. His intention and that of the Provisional Government was to effect a total separation from *England*, but not to let the country become the dependent of *France*.

After several other observations, in which Mr. *Emmet* strenuously endeavoured to vindicate his conduct and that of the Provisional Government, he was interrupted by *Lord Norbury*, who informed him that he had instead of offering any thing in stay of sentence in point of law, proceeded in a manner the most unbecoming a man in his situation, and had broached treason the most abominable.

Mr. *Emmet* answered, that he understood it was the duty of a judge, when a prisoner was convicted to pronounce the sentence of the law: that the judge he also understood sometimes thought it his duty, not only to pass sentence, but to deliver an exhortation to the prisoner, and pass his opinion as to the motives by which the prisoner was actuated. Where were the boasted laws of the country, if an unfortunate prisoner, just about to be delivered into the hands of the executioner was not suffered to vindicate his motives of action.

Mr. *Emmet* having proceeded much further in his own vindication was again interrupted by the Court, and informed by Lord *Norbury*, that as he had not offered any thing in point of law to stay the sentence, it was an imperative and painful duty now to be performed: that he had been suffered to go on, although in almost every word, he had uttered treason more extensive than even the indictment had charged against him; that he had been heard with a patience which was not to be met with in the report of any trial which had taken place in this or any other country.

Mr. *Emmet* said, my Lord I have but a few words more. I am now going to my cold and silent grave. I have but one request—Let no Epitaph be upon my tomb—no man can write my Epitaph—I am not permitted to vindicate my character.—No man now dare vindicate my character. When my country takes her place amongst the nations of the earth, then and then only can my character be vindicated: then only may my Epitaph be written—I am done.

REPORT OF THE TRIAL OF ROBERT EMMET, UPON AN INDICTMENT FOR HIGH TREASON

DUBLIN, 1803

DOWNPATRICK

REPORT OF THE TRIAL OF THOMAS RUSSELL,
A REBEL GENERAL DURING
THE LATE INSURRECTION

Downpatrick, October 20, 1803

YESTERDAY morning, at ten o'clock, the court met pursuant to adjournment, when Thomas Russel was put to the bar, charged with high treason, under the statute of 25 Edward III.

The prisoner and the crown mutually waving their right to challenge, the following gentlemen were sworn of the jury, viz.

Sir J. Bristow, foreman. T. Douglas, esq., T. Waring, esq., H. Kennedy, esq., R. Thompson, esq., E.S. Ruthven, esq., I. Cleland, esq., J. Moore, esq., C. Skinner, esq., C.H. Moore, esq., A. Crawford, esq., T. Potter, esq.

The attorney general opened the case, in a very eloquent and able speech of considerable length, recapitulating the crimes with which the prisoner stood charged . . .

Wm. Cosby, of Saintfield, county Down, sworn. Is a yeoman in capt. Price's corps; recollected hiring a horse on the Friday of the last races, 22nd July, to James Drake, to go to Annadown, or the Cross-roads; identified the prisoner, whom he saw same day; Drake promised to pay him; Russel paid him for the horse; it was 10 o'clock in the morning. Cross-examined. He thinks it was the prisoner paid 3s. 3d.

Robert Nelson sworn. Is acquainted with James Drake; saw him on the Friday of the races coming Ballinahinch road; knows James Smith's house at Annadown; it was about 400 perch from Smith's house, he saw Drake riding with another man; Drake's horse was brought back by a little boy.

James Keenan sworn. Lives at the winning post on the race ground, he recollected the Maze races; heard that there was to be a rising on the 23rd July; on the Friday of the races heard of a meeting to be at Smith's of Annadown; was at the meeting; saw some whom he knew; there were about nine men there drinking whiskey; and among them James Drake, James Corry, and Hugh M'Mullen; M'Mullen told him of the meeting; saw some he would not know; saw the prisoner there; he sat down; the prisoner asked him what he could do in respect to rebellion; he said that there were about ten men in his village, but that if he spoke to them about rebellion, they would hit him in the face; the prisoner then said that he believed he might go out of the country as that was the case, but that the rebellion must go on in other places, as he could not stop it. He saw an uniform of green cloth, with epaulets and lace; the prisoner desired Drake to put on the uniform, but he refused; the prisoner put it on himself for a few minutes, and then took it off himself, and thinks it was tied up in a cloth. He recollected a stranger coming in at that time to the room, and the prisoner asked the stranger what he could do about raising men for rebellion? the stranger said he could raise about 150 men; recollects Corry saying on leaving the room, that he would go and try what he could do in Downpatrick . . .

Major Sirr sworn and examined; proved he arrested the prisoner in arms, and that he pulled out pistols on him.

The proclamation was then read as before, where hostages were to be taken.

The evidence for the crown having been closed, the prisoner declined calling any witnesses in his defence, and allowed the case to go to the jury on such evidence as had been adduced on the part of the crown.

The hon. baron George, with his usual ability and precision, recapitulated the evidence which had been adduced; and the jury having retired only for a few minutes, returned a verdict of GUILTY, against the prisoner . . .

The learned judge then pronounced the awful sentence of the law, which the prisoner listened to with the greatest composure, bowed respectfully to the court, and then retired in custody of the sheriff.

WALKER'S HIBERNIAN MAGAZINE, OCTOBER 1803

FEW, FEW HAVE I KNOWN LIKE HIM

Wednesday, Cabin Hill, Belfast—"I have not been in Belfast these six weeks. The subject there of late would have been very painful. *Now* I find it is mostly pity and admiration. To the last moment Russell's fortitude was conspicuous, his speech was eloquent and affecting. A Mr. Cole, a relation of the Kennedys and also of Russell's, repeated it, word for word, at Doctor Mattear's, as he said he never, never could forget it, the appearance, manner and voice of the man who uttered it. D. G[ordon] sat beside him, and as he had notes of his speech he either dropped or lost one (which, I suppose, was the occasion of what was called embarrassment). He said there would be a wrong account of it, and pointed out to Gordon the cause. The judge remarked (for he answered him) that he was sorry to hear him say he gloried in what he had done. He denied the word *glory*, and to the other observations of the judge he always bowed. There was no answer returned to his request of a few days at the time, but when he returned to prison he was told it would not be granted. The next morning Fulton was sent to him . . . He received the Sacrament *twice* and went with him, bowed to some gentlemen he passed, and gave them his good wishes, directed the hangman in his office and put the rope round his neck himself. Gordon saw the book and the *letter* he left for his sister—affectionate and grateful and religious. Enthusiastic he did indeed appear; religious, he always was since I knew him, and in his late confinement it was not to be wondered at that such a mind as his might have grown even flighty. I rejoice in it, and that whatever it was— enthusiasm, fortitude or error— that it bore him up to the last. Few, few have I known like him."

LETTER FROM MRS MARTHA McTIER TO DR WILLIAM DRENNAN, *c.* 25 OCTOBER 1803

THOMAS RUSSELL

INDEX

Abbot, Charles, Lord Colchester, 191 (*illus.*)
  extract from diary of, 191–2
An Act for the Relief of His Majesty's Popish
  or Roman Catholic Subjects of Ireland
  (1793), 3, 37–9
Act of Union (1801), 7, 182–4; *see also* union
  between Great Britain and Ireland
Adams, James, 101
Addington, Mr, 187
Admiral, 89
agrarian unrest, 3, 4, 5
Alexander, John, 96
America, 40, 41
  Tone's departure for (1795), 4, 60
Annadown (Co. Down), 207
Antrim (county), 129
  rebellion in, 133, 135–6
Antrim (town), 135–6
Ardouin, General, 161
Arklow (Co. Wicklow), 127, 192
Armagh (city)
  meeting of Orange Societies of Ulster
  (1797), 99–100
Armagh (county), 171
  disturbances and rioting: 1795, 63–4; 1796,
  71
armed revolution, 2; *see also* rebellion of 1798
Armstrong, Robert, 100, 103
Athy assizes
  treason indictments (1795), 62
Atkinson, Mr (High Constable of Belfast), 96
Azemard, General, 161

Babbin, Captain, 161
Bagenal, Mrs, 203
Ballentine, John, 102
Ballina (Co. Mayo)
  French army in, 152, 160, 161
Ballymena (Co. Antrim), 133
Ballynahinch (Co. Down), 142
Bantry Bay (Co. Cork)
  French invasion fleet (1796), 5, 87–90
Barber, Colonel, 91, 96, 100
Barclay's Tavern (Belfast), 1
Barret, John, 93
Bayham, Lord, 35

Bedout, Captain, 85, 89, 90
Belfast, 4, 135
  Falls Road forge, capture of (1797), 100–1
Belfast News-Letter, 2
Belfast Society for Promoting Knowledge, 5
Belfast Yeomanry Cavalry, 135
Bell, George, 71
Bellew, Christopher, 31
Beresford, Mr, 51
Betau, Lieutenant, 173
Bishop, William and Thomas (of
      Ballymorrie), 150
Blessington (Co. Wicklow), 127
Bond, Oliver, 3, 6, 114
  imprisonment, 44
Boreland, James, 103
Boyd, Judge, 84
Boyle, John, 50
Boyle (Co. Roscommon), 43
Braughall, Tom, 136
Break-of-Day Men, 63
Bridport, Lord, 91
Bristow, Sir J., 207
Bristow, Rev. William, 105
Browne, Colonel, 8, 199
Browne, Wogan, 44
Brush, Captain, 93
Buonaparte, Napoleon, 194
  meeting with Tone (1797), 107
Burke, Dr, 28
Burke, Edmund
  Reflections on the Revolution in France, 2
Burnside, James, 93
Burrows, Rev. Mr (Kyle), 127
Butler, Simon, 3, 22, 28, 40
  imprisonment, 44
Byrne, Edward, 31
Byrne, P. (printer), 137
Byrne, Patrick, 122
Byrnes, Peter, 103

Callwell, R., 50
Camden, Lord, 73 (*illus.*), 139
Campbell, Mr, 103
Carlow (county), 126, 137
Carnot, 5, 67–8

212 Carrickfergus (Co. Antrim)
          General Court Martial (August 1798),
              152
       Carrickfergus Castle, 151 (*illus.*)
       Carrickfergus Gaol, 106
       Castlebar (Co. Mayo)
          French army in, 153, 161
       Castledermot (Co. Kildare), 137
       Castlereagh, Lord, 5, 6, 7, 35, 81, 135, 159,
              171, 177 (*illus.*), 189, 193
          Cornwallis's praise of, 146, 158
          rebellion of 1803, account of, 195–200
          rebellion of 1798, reports on, 126, 129, 138,
              166
       Catholic Committee, 1, 3, 28, 74
       Catholic Emancipation, 95, 98, 119, 159
          demands for, 1, 2, 3, 21; Catholic petition
              (1793), 31–2; Tone's *Argument on Behalf of
              the Catholics of Ireland* (1791), 1, 18–20
          Grattan's bill (1796), 55–6
          opposition to, 2; George III, 8, 189–90;
              Protestant fears of forfeiture, 2–3, 27
          recall of Lord Fitzwilliam (1795), 4
          Relief Act (1793), 37–9
       Catholic Relief Act (1793), 3, 37–9
          reaction to, 40–2
       Catholic secret societies *see* Defenders
       Cavan (county), 46
       Chambers, Mr, 137
       Charlemont, Lord, 27
       Cherin, General, 88, 89
       Chetwynd, Captain, 133
       Clain (Clane, Co. Kildare), 137
       Clare, Lord, 159, 176 (*illus.*)
          promotion of, 176–7
       Clare (county), 171
       Clarke, Alexander, 93
       Clarke, Mr, 74, 76
       Clavering, Colonel, 128, 133, 135, 136
       Clewlow, Rev. (of Saintfield), 149
       Clifden, Lord, 97–8
       Clonmel (Co. Tipperary)
          Society of the United Irishmen, 28
       Clonmell, Lord, 51
       Cochran, John, 82
       Colchester, Lord, 97
       Colclough, John (of Balliteigue), 140
       Cole, Mr, 208
       Coleraine (Co. Londonderry), 80

Committee of Secrecy
    report of, 94–7
Connaught mail
    stopping of, 126
Connolly, Thomas, 171
Cooke, Edward, 132, 139, 153–4
Cooper, Samuel, 140
Cork Legion of Volunteers, 91
Cork Militia, 137
Cornwallis, Lord (Lord Lieutenant), 7, 8,
        167 (*illus.*)
    appointment, 98, 119
    arrival in Dublin (June 1798), 141
    Catholic Emancipation, on, 190
    future government, proposals for, 157–8
    promotion of Lord Clare, on, 176–7
    rebellion of 1798, reports on, 123, 162, 173–
        74, 175; excesses of militia and yeomanry,
        143–4, 145, 148–49, 150–1; French in
        Mayo, 152, 153; invitation to surrender,
        150–1
    union between Great Britain and Ireland,
        158, 163–5, 167; negotiation of, 7, 175,
        181
corruption, 7, 175
Corry, Isaac, 7, 181
Corry, James, 207
Cosby, William, 207
Coulter, Thomas (of Lecale, Co. Down), 149
Cradock, Major-General, 156
Crawford, A., 207
Crawford, Dr, 6, 93
Croaghan (Co. Wicklow), 192
Crosbie, Major-General, 42
Curran, Mr, 103, 136

Darnley, Lord, 181
Davison, Abraham, 100
De Clifford, Lord, 181
De Latocnaye
    tour of Ireland (1796–1797), 80–1
De Sombrieul, Count, 166
*Declaration and Resolutions of the United Irishmen
        of Belfast* (1791), 1–2, 3, 20–1
Declaration of the Rights of Man and of Citizens
        (National Assembly of France), 2, 16–18
Defenders, 3, 4, 5, 46, 62, 113, 198
    battles with Peep o' Day Boys and
        Orangemen, 63–4, 71

Dessaix, General, 78, 106, 107
detention, 17
Devereux, James Edward, 31
Dickson, Dr, 40
Dillon, John, 120
Dillon, Thomas, 120
Dixon, Mr (of Castlebridge), 140
Dnrivak, Captain, 161
Dobbyn, Rev. Dr (Finglas), 148
Donelly, Joseph, 120
Donnegor-Hill (Donegore Hill, Co. Antrim), 128
Donoughmore, Lord, 91
Doris, 162 (*illus.*), 163
Douglas, T., 207
Down (county)
    arrests of United Irishmen (1796), 102
    manufacture of pikes, 171
    rebellion of 1798, 129
Downes, Mr Justice, 51
Downpatrick (Co. Down), 206 (*illus.*)
    assizes (July 1798), 149–50
Downshire, Marquis of, 117, 127, 181
Doyle, James, 120
Doyle, Mr, 202–3
Drake, James, 207
Drennan, Dr William, 13 (*illus.*), 30, 209
    plan for founding of secret society (1791), 1, 13–14
    resignation from United Irishmen, 3–4
Dromore (Co. Down)
    murder of Macdowell (1797), 93
Dublin
    curfew notice (24 May 1798), 121
    militia, 97
    rebellion of 1798, 144
    rebellion of 1803, 195
    Society of the United Irishmen, 22–3
Dufour, General, 161
Duignan, Dr, 56
Dundalk Yeomanry, 97
Dundas, Henry, 189 (*illus.*), 189–90
    Plan for Providing more Completely for the Security of the Country (1794), 49–50
Durham, Colonel, 135, 136
Dwyer, Michael, 7
    escape of (1799), 172–3

Edenfor, Lieutenant, 133

Edgworth, M., 34
Egan, Mr, 178
Elliot, Rev., 41
Ellison, Lieutenant, 96
Ely, Lord, 176
Emmet, Robert, 8, 45, 114, 192, 196 (*illus.*), 201 (*illus.*)
    insurrection of 1803, 195–200
    trial of, 200–4; speech from the dock, 204–6
Emmet, Thomas Addis, 196
English rule, 19, 20, 95–6
Enniscorthy (Co. Wexford), 128, 138
Enniskillen (Co. Fermanagh), 41, 43, 46
equality, 2, 9, 16, 17, 21
Ethalion, 163
European Enlightenment, 2
European war *see* war with France
'The Exiled Irishman's Lamentation' (song), 56–7

Fallen, William, 103
Felony Act (1796), 76–7
Ferns (Co. Wexford), 128
Fife Fencibles, 103
Finucane, Mr Justice, 62
Fitzgerald, Lord Edward, 6, 7, 114, 127
    arrest of (May 1798), 6, 120 (*illus.*), 121
    death of, 136, 137
    plans for 1798 rebellion, 114–16
Fitzgibbon, Lord, 51
Fitzsimmons, William, 62
Fitzwilliam, Lord (Lord Lieutenant), 51–2
    Protestant Dissenters' Address to (January 1795), 55
    recall of (February 1795), 4, 58
Flack, Mr, 93
Floyd, Lieutenant-General, 191
Fontaine, General, 160, 161
Forbes, Mr, 52
Fox, Mr, 96, 100, 178
France; *see also* French Revolution
    European war *see* war with France
    invasion attempts *see* French invasions
    National Assembly, 15, 16; *Declaration of the Rights of Man and of Citizens*, 16–18
    Robert Emmet and, 192, 204–5
    Tone's arrival in (1796), 64–8
Fraternité (French frigate), 86, 87
freedom of expression, 17

214   freedom of religion, 17

Freemasonry, 13

French, Sir Thomas, 31

French agents

trial of Rev. William Jackson (1795), 4, 60

French invasions

anticipation of invasion, 5, 62; security
measures, 49–50

1796 attempt, 5; Tone in France, 64–8, 74–
6; defence preparations, 82–4, 91; progress
of the fleet, 85–90; Bantry Bay, 87–90

1797–1798: Tone's preparations, 106–7,
114; Ballina taken, 152; 'Castlebar affair',
153–4; Mayo Manifesto, 155; surrender,
156–7; Humbert's report to Executive
Directory, 160–2; arrival of *La Hoche* in
Lough Swilly, 163

1801 expectations, 191

French Revolution, 2, 3, 15–16, 46, 81

Declaration of the Rights of Man and of Citizens,
2, 16–18

treatment of Louis XVI: dethronement, 29–
30; trial, 32–3; execution, 33–5

fundamental rights *see* rights of man

Galway (county)

manufacture of pikes, 171

Gamble, Rev. Mr (Ordinary of Newgate),
148

George, Baron, 208

George III, 8, 36 (*illus.*)

Catholic Emancipation, opposition to,
189–90

union between Great Britain and Ireland:
speech at opening session of first
Parliament, 187–9

war with France, and, 36–7, 193

Glengarry Regiment, 172

Glenny, F., 101

'Gog' *see* Keogh, John

Goldie, General M., 136

Goldrisk (Commissary), 154

Gordon, D., 208

Gordon, Mr, 101

Gorey (Co. Wexford), 127

government of Ireland

lack of national government, 19, 20

Grammont, Captain, 87

Granard, Lord, 154

Grangemore (near Portadown, Co. Armagh),
64

Grattan, Henry, MP, 41, 52, 178 (*illus.*)

Catholic Emancipation bill (1795), 55–6

union between Great Britain and Ireland:
speech to House of Commons (January
1800), 178–80, 181

wounding of Isaac Corry (1800), 7

Grenville, Lord, 85, 189

Grier, James, 93

Griffin, Michael, 62

Griffith, Mr, 44

Grogan, Mr, 139

Grouchy, General, 87, 88–9

Hacketstown (Co. Carlow), 172

Haffey, James, 93

Hamilton, Mr, 196

Harold's Cross (Dublin), 203

Harris, Mr, 101

Harrison, John, 93

Hart, William, 195

Harvey, Bagenal, 7, 139–40

Haslett, Henry, 50, 81

Haslett, John, 50

Hawkesbury, Lord, 187

Hay, Edward (of Ballinkeel), 140

Hay, John, 7

Heasty, Robert, 149

Hedouville, General, 106

Hewett, Major-General, 154

Hewitt, G., 121

Hibernian Journal, 171

Higgins, Andrew, 62

highwaymen, 151, 158

Hoche, General Lazarre, 67, 83 (*illus.*), 107

meeting with Tone (1796), 74, 76

Holt, Joseph, 7, 158

Horan, Barth., 62

House of Commons, 22, 178

House of Lords

debate on state of Ireland (March 1798),
116–19

Huete, Captain, 161

Hughes, Mr (of Ballytrant), 140

human rights *see* rights of man

Humbert, General

report to Executive Directory (August
1798), 160–2

surrender to General Lake, 156 (*illus.*)

Huntley, Lord, 151
Hutchins, Mr, 89
'Hutton, Mr' *see* Tone, Theobald Wolfe

Immortalité, 88
independence of Ireland, 13, 60
Indomptable, 5, 85, 89
informers and information, 6, 69, 101, 130–2
innocence, presumption of, 17

Jackson, Thomas, 93, 114
Jackson, Rev. William (French agent)
   trial for high treason (1795), 4, 60
Jacobins, 29, 143
Johnson, Captain, 130
Jones, William Todd, MP, 28, 40
   Protestant fears of land forfeiture, on, 3, 27
Jourdan, M., 67

Kane, Roger, 120
Karr, James, 120
Keane, William, 93
Keenan, James, 207
   arrest, 5
   committal (1796), 84
Kelburn, Rev. Sinclair, 6, 93
Kelly, Denis, 62
Kennedy, H., 207
Kennedy, John, 93
Kennedy, Mr (printer), 81
Keogh, John ('Gog'), 31, 32 (*illus.*), 45
Keogh, Mr, 137
Ker, Lieutenant-Colonel, 135
Kerfoot, George, 120
Keugh, Mathew, 139, 140
Kilcullen (Co. Kildare), 137
Kildare (county)
   rebellion of 1798, 126, 144, 145, 148, 150
Killala Bay (Co. Mayo), 163
   French in, 152, 160, 162
Kilmainham Barracks (Dublin), 94 (*illus.*)
Kilmainham Gaol (Dublin)
   imprisonment of United Irishmen (1797),
   93
Kilwarden, Lord (Arthur Wolfe,
   1st Viscount), 8, 199
King, Thomas, 62
Kingsmill, Robert, 132
Kinselagh, John, 120

Kirkwood, Hugh, 93
Knox, General, 128

La Croix, Charles de, 65
La Fayette, Marquis de, 15, 29
La Hoche, 162 (*illus.*)
   arrival in Lough Swilly (1798), 163
Lake, Lieutenant-General, 100, 121, 138, 153,
   154
   defeat of the French, 156–7
   surrender of General Humbert to, 156
   (*illus.*)
Lamare, M., 65
Lambert (brigadier-general in French army),
   78
land forfeiture and redistribution
   Protestant fears of, 2–3, 27
law, 17
   equality, 17
   expression of the will of the community, 17
Lawless, Mr, 136, 197
lawless desperados, 158
Lawson, Mr (bookseller), 101
Lecourbe (brigadier-general in French army),
   78
Ledwich, Mr, 137
Légion des Francs, 88
Lewines, Mr, 107
Limerick (county), 119, 191
Limerick, Bishop of, 172
Lindsay, John, 103
Littlehales, E.B., 177, 193–4
Loftus, General, 165
Louis XVI, King of France, 15–16
   dethronement, 29–30
   trial and execution, 3, 32–3, 33–5
Lumley, Lieutenant-Colonel, 135, 136

McAlister, John, 103
M'Anally, James, 102
McArt's fort (Cave Hill, Belfast), 4
McCabe, William, 42, 50
M'Cleverty, Mr, 128
McClure, John, 101
M'Cormick, Richard ('Magog'), 28, 40, 42,
   44, 45–6, 114
McCracken, Henry Joy, 4, 5, 7, 146 (*illus.*)
   committal on charge of high treason (1796),
   84

court-martial (July 1798), 147
McCracken, William, 93
McCullough, Mr, 44
M'Donnell, Captain, 172–3
Macdowell, Mr (Orangeman), 93
McIlveen, Gilbert, 1, 50
M'Kenna, Dr, 28
M'Kiernan, Patrick, 71
McLoughlin, Mr, 46
McManus, William, 93
M'Mullen, Hugh, 207
M'Nally, Leonard, 28
MacNally, Mr, 203
Macnevin, Mr, 114, 196, 197
McTier, Martha, 8, 208–9
McTier, Samuel, 1, 208
Madgett, Mr, 66, 67, 68, 85
Magee, Dr Robert, 103
Magee, William, 50
'Magog' see M'Cormick, Richard
Magrath, Mr, 120
Maguire, Simon, 28
Malmesbury, Lord, 5, 85
Manorhamilton (Co. Leitrim), 43
maps
    map of Europe (Northern Star, 1796), 79
        (illus.)
    map of Ireland, 75 (illus.)
Marie Antoinette, Queen of France, 45 (illus.)
martial law, 6, 121, 124, 148–9, 191
Mattear, Dr see McTier, Samuel
May, Mr, 177
Mayo (county)
    rebellion of 1798, 166; French invasion,
        155–63
Mayo Manifesto, 155
Meath (county)
    rebellion of 1798, 126, 144, 145
Melling, Mr, 101
Military Road (Co. Wicklow), 191–2
militia, 43, 48, 49, 97, 145
    excesses of, 149, 153
Milltown, Earl of, 127
Moan, James, 71
Moira, Earl of, 116–17
Monaghan (county), 46
Monaghan Militia, 100, 135
    execution of four militiamen (1797), 98–9
Monasterevan (Co. Kildare), 137

Monroe, James (American ambassador in
    France), 64–5, 68
Moore, Arthur, 178
Moore, Mr, 151
Moore, Mr (president of the Connaught
    Directory), 166
Morrison, Hugh, 82
Mount Cashel, Stephen, 2nd Earl, 8, 192, 192
    (illus.)
Mountjoy, Lord, 133 (illus.)
Mulligan, William, 103
Munro, Henry, 7, 141 (illus.)
Murdoch, Bob, 132
Murphy, Fr, 192
Murphy, James, 120

Naas (Co. Kildare), 137
nation, as source of all sovereignty, 2, 16–17
national government, 19, 20
Navan (Co. Meath), 46
Needham, General, 192
Neilson, Robert, 93
Neilson, Samuel, 1, 4, 5, 40, 42, 50, 123 (illus.)
    arrest of (1796), 81–2
    committal for high treason (1798), 124
Nelson, Robert, 207
Newell, Edward John, 6, 130 (illus.), 130–2
Newry (Co. Down), 101
Newtown Mount-Kennedy (Co. Wicklow),
    127
Nicholson, Jacob, 93
Norbury, Lord, 200, 204, 205
North Mayo Militia, 62, 63
Northern Mail Coach
    burning of (1798), 125–6
Northern Star, 3, 40
    French Revolution and European war,
        reporting of, 3, 5
    seditious libel, prosecution for (1794), 3,
        50–1
    seizure and occupation (1797), 91–2; arrest
        of proprietors, 91–2; printing press
        destroyed, 6
Nugent, General G., 71, 128, 133, 135, 154
Nunn, Rev. Joshua, 128

oaths, administering and taking of
    Felony Act (1796), 76–7
    trial of William Orr (1797), 103–4, 105

O'Brien, Peter, 120
O'Connor, Arthur, 91, 92
O'Connor, Laurance, 62, 197
Offaly (King's County)
    rebellion of 1798 in, 126, 127
Ogle, Mr, 56
O'Neil, Mears, 46
O'Neill, Lord Viscount, 103, 133 (*illus.*)
Orange Order, 5, 6; *see also* Orangemen
    address of Masters of Orange Societies in
        Antrim (1803), 194–5
    aims of, 4, 99
    founding of (1795), 4, 64
    opposition to United Irishmen, 70–1, 99
    Resolutions of the Orange Societies of
        Ulster (Armagh, 1797), 99–100
Orangemen, 93, 132, 154
    capital convictions (1796), 71
Ormonde, Lord, 154
Orr, Samuel, 103
Orr, William, 6
    arrest of (1796), 82
    dying declaration of, 104–6
    trial of (1797), 103–4, 105
    'Wake of William Orr', 111–13
Osborne, Mr, 81

'P.P.' *see* Russell, Thomas
Paine, Thomas
    The Rights of Man (1791), 2, 14–18
Palmer, Mr, 202
papists; *see also* Catholic Emancipation
    Catholic Relief Act (1793), 37–9
parliamentary reform
    demands for, 1, 2, 3, 18–23, 69–70, 81, 95;
        *Declaration and Resolutions of the United
        Irishmen* (1791), 1, 20–1; Tone's *Argument
        on Behalf of the Catholics of Ireland* (1791),
        18–20
    Scotland, 30–1
Peep o' Day Boys, 4
    battles with Defenders (1795), 63–4
Pelham, Mr, 94
Penal Laws, 1
people, sovereignty of, 33
Pichegru, M., 67
pikes, 101
    manufacture of, 171–2; capture of Falls
        Road forge (Belfast, 1797), 100–1

Pitt, William, 2, 51, 159, 189
    French invasion, preparations for, 82–4
polarisation of Irish society, 4, 9
political bigotry, 2, 9, 19, 21
political liberty, 17
Ponsonby, Mr, 52
Ponsonby, W.B., 178
Portadown (Co. Armagh), 64
Portaferry (Co. Down), 141
Portland, Duke of, 135, 143, 146, 152, 158,
    159, 163–5, 167
Potter, T., 207
Presbyterians, 1
property rights, 18
Prosheau, Lieutenant G., 90 (*illus.*)
Prosperous (Co. Kildare), 137
Protestant Ascendancy
    fears of forfeiture, 2–3, 27
Protestant Dissenters
    address to Lord Fitzwilliam (1795), 55
Protestant religion
    ascendancy of, 172
Protestant societies
    Orange Order, 4, 64, 71, 99–100
    Peep o' Day Boys, 4, 64
Protestants
    Wexford massacre, 127–8
public contributions, 18
public force, 17

Queery, John (of Belfast), 152
Quigley, Mr, 196, 197

Rabb, John, 50
Raccou, Captain, 161
Rastadt, battle of, 78
Rathmines (Co. Dublin), 137
rebellion of 1798, 113
    preparations and counter-measures, 6,
        113, 114–19; French invasion plans, 106–
        7, 114; Limerick proclaimed, 119; seizure
        of plans for rebellion, 6, 136; arrests of
        leaders, 6, 114, 120, 121, 122, 136–7;
        curfew in Dublin, 121
    hostilities, 6, 7, 123–54; Northern Mail
        Coach stopped, 125–6; martial law, 6,
        121, 124; arrival of Lord Cornwallis (June
        1798), 141; excesses of militia and
        yeomanry, 143, 144, 149

local uprisings: Antrim, 129, 133, 135–6; Down, 129; Kildare, 126, 137, 145, 148, 150; Meath, 126, 144–5; North generally, 124, 128, 129, 133, 135–6, 141; Wexford, 129, 137, 138–40, 142; Wicklow, 126, 127

decline and aftermath, 7, 144–67; proclamation of general pardon, 145–6; court-martial of Henry Joy McCracken (July 1798), 147; execution of Sheares brothers (July 1798), 148–9; 'no law but martial law', 148–9; Downpatrick assizes, 149–50; guerrilla warfare, 7, 143, 144–5, 166; general court-martial at Carrickfergus, 152; highwaymen and desperados, 151, 158; trial and death of Tone, 7, 165–6

French in Mayo: Mayo Manifesto (September 1798), 155; surrender of the French, 156–7; Humbert's account, 160–2; *La Hoche* in Lough Swilly, 163

rebellion of 1803, 8, 195–200
provisional government, 201, 204, 205
trial of Robert Emmet, 200–4; speech from the dock, 204–6
trial of Thomas Russell, 206–8

Reilly, James, 120

religious bigotry, 2, 9, 19, 21, 28

republicanism, 3, 13, 40, 42

revolutionary movement
transformation of United Irishmen into, 4

Reynolds, Thomas, 6, 44, 45, 95 (*illus.*)

Rhine army, 78–80

Rice, Dominick, 28

Richardson, Mr, 80, 81

rights of man, 2, 9, 20, 21
Declaration of the Rights of Man and of Citizens (France), 2, 16–18
Paine's *The Rights of Man* (1791), 2, 14–18
political philosophy of United Irishmen, 2

rioting, 43
Armagh, 63–4

Roach, Mr, 139

Roar (Co. Kilkenny), 142

Robespierre, 46, 92

Robuste, 163

Roden, Lord, 154, 156

Ross, Major-General, 119, 123, 132, 143, 149, 151, 162, 173, 190

Rotze, General, 76

Rowan, Archibald Hamilton, 28, 28 (*illus.*), 30, 44, 45, 66
trial and conviction of, 3, 48–9

Russborough estate (Co. Wicklow), 127

Russell, Thomas ('P. P.'), 1, 3, 4, 5, 8, 40 (*illus.*), 41, 42, 43, 45, 46, 209 (*illus.*)
arrest of (1796), 81–2
journal extracts, 1793–1794: April–May 1793, 40–3; December 1793–January 1794, 44–6
rebellion of 1803, involvement in, 196, 197, 198
trial of (December 1803), 8, 206–8

Ruthven, R.S., 207

Ruty, Captain, 161

Ryan, Captain Daniel Frederick, 121, 127

Ryan, Dr, 46

Ryans, Christopher, 103

Sadlier, Thomas, 28

St Cyr, General, 78

Sampson, Mr, 114

Santerre, Mareschal, 34

Sarrazin, General, 160, 161
Mayo Manifesto (September 1798), 155

Scotland, 30–1, 59

secrecy, 13, 72

secret societies *see* Defenders; Orange Order; Peep o' Day Boys; United Irishmen

sectarian hatred, 5

Seddon, Major, 133

Séduisant (French frigate), 86

separation of powers, 18

Shannon, Lord, 166

Shannon, Mr, 81

Sheares, Henry, 147 (*illus.*)
arrest of, 6, 122
execution of (July 1798), 7, 148–9

Sheares, John, 148 (*illus.*)
arrest of, 6, 122
execution of (July 1798), 7, 148–9

Simms, Robert and William, 1, 4, 50
arrest of (1797), 91–2

Sinclair, William, 1

Sirr, Major, 203, 207

Skelly, John (of Creevy Tennant), 149–50

Sligo, 154

Sloan, James, 99

Smith, James (of Annadown), 207

Smith, James (Orangeman), 71
Smith, James (Tone's alias), 65, 68
Smith, Major, 135
Smith, Matthew, 92
Smith, Sir Sydney, 76
Society of the United Irishmen *see* United
  Irishmen
sovereignty
  nation as source of, 2, 16–17
  people, of, 33
Sparks, Ensign, 133
Spear, Henry, 93
Spencer, Earl, 189
Stafford, Mr (of Skreene), 140
Stapelton, Colonel, 133
Stewart, Sir James, 139
Stewart, Robert, *see* Castlereagh, Lord
Stokes, Mr, 46
Stradbally (Queen's County/Laois), 113
Surazin, General *see* Sarrazin, General
Swan, Mr Justice, 121
Swayne, Captain, 122 (*illus.*)
Sweetman, Dr, 114
Sweetman, E., 46
Sweetman, John, 45
Swift, Jonathan, 175
Switzerland, 205

Talbot, William (of Castle-Talbot), 140
Tallaght (Co. Dublin), 202
Tandy, James Napper, 22 (*illus.*), 22–3
Taponier, General, 78
taxes, 81
Taylor, Brigadier-General, 152
Taylor's map of Ireland, 107
Teeling, Mr, 81
Templeton, George, 102
Templeton, John, 102
Templeton, William, 93
Tennant, Mr, 107
Tennent, William, 1, 50
Thompson, R., 207
Thompson, Thomas, 102
Tipperary (county),
  rebellion, 150
Tisdall, John, 50
tithes, 158
Toland, Daniel, 93
Tone, Matthew, 106

Tone, Theobald Wolfe ('Mr Hutton'), 1, 28,
  40, 41, 42, 44, 45, 46, 65 (*illus.*), 165 (*illus.*)
  Catholic Emancipation, and: *An Argument*
    on Behalf of the Catholics of Ireland (1791), 1,
    18–20
  Declaration and Resolutions of the United
    Irishmen of Belfast (1791), 1–2, 3, 20–1
  departure for America (1795), 4, 60
  French assistance, and, 85–90; 1796, 5, 64–8,
    74–6; 1797–1798, 106–7, 114, 163;
    meeting with Carnot, 67–8; meeting with
    Hoche, 74, 76
  journal extracts: 1796 - 33rd birthday, 73;
    June 1798, 136–7
  Lord Edward Fitzgerald's death, and, 136–7
  separation from England, and, 95–6
  suicide of, 7, 166
  trial of, 165–6
Toomebridge (Co. Antrim), 133
Touffaint, Captain, 161
Townsley, Thomas (of Balloo), 150
Tullamore (Co. Offaly), 127
Turner, Rev. Mr (of Ballingale), 127–8
union between Great Britain and Ireland
  proposals for union, 7, 35, 59, 159;
    Cornwallis's views, 7, 158, 173–4, 175;
    government determination to press ahead
    (1798), 167; heads of the Treaty of Union
    (1798), 163–5; debate, 171, 172;
    opposition, 59, 171, 173–5, 178–80;
    Grattan's speech (January 1800), 178–80;
    negotiations, 7, 175
  legislation, 181; Act of Union (1801), 7,
    182–4; meeting of imperial parliament
    (January 1801), 8, 187–9
union of people of Ireland, 21, 22, 61, 70–1
Unite, Lieutenant, 133
'Unite and Be Free' (song), 61
United Irishmen; *see also* Tone, Theobald
  Wolfe
  foundation and early years (1791–1793),
    1–3, 13–21; Drennan's vision, 1, 13–14;
    Declaration of the Rights of Man, 14–18;
    Tone's arguments (1791), 18–20, 95–6;
    founding members, 1; *Declaration and*
    Resolutions (1791), 1–2, 3, 20–1;
    propaganda campaign, 2; Dublin
    Society, 22–3; Clonmel Society, 28;
    Address to the Delegates for Promoting a

Reform in Scotland (1792), 30–1
1794–1795: transformation into revolutionary movement, 40–6; government clampdown, 3–4, 44, 48, 50–1, 60; Tone's departure for America (1795), 4, 60; foundation of Orange Order, 4
1796–1797: arrests of leaders, 5, 6, 81–2, 92, 93, 102–3; French invasion attempt (1796), 5–6, 64–8, 74–6, 85–91; Felony Act, 76–7; seizure of *Northern Star* (1797), 6, 91–2; report of Committee of Secrecy, 94–7; hostilities (1797), 97–8; trial of William Orr (1797), 103–6
1797–1798: French invasion preparations, 106–7, 114; plans for rebellion, 6, 114–16; House of Lords debate on state of Ireland, 116–19; further arrests, 120–1, 122; hostilities, 123–54. *see further* rebellion of 1798
1803 rebellion, 8; *see further* rebellion of 1803; deaths of Emmet and Russell, 8
political philosophy: twin demands: parliamentary reform and Catholic Emancipation, 1, 2, 3, 18–23, 95; agrarian undercurrent, 2–3, 27; rights of man, 2, 14–18; union of people of Ireland, 21, 22
newspaper *see Northern Star*
signs of the Society, 103

Venek, General, 76
Verner, Mr, 63
volunteer cavalry, 49–50, 91
volunteer companies, 49, 91, 141

'Wake of William Orr', 111–13
Walker, Mr, 101
Walker, Samuel, 103

Walpole, Colonel, 137
war with France, 3, 8, 41–2, 47–8, 78–80
Declaration of War (1793): George III's message, 36–7
defence measures: Plan for Providing more Completely for the Security of the Country (1794), 49–50
hopes of France disappointed (1794), 47–8
temporary suspension of hostilities (1801), 8
Waring, T., 207
Warren, Sir J.B., 47
Watkin's Ancient British Fencibles, 97
Watt, Gawen (of Belfast), 152
Waudre, Colonel, 88
Wexford (county)
rebellion of 1798, 3, 126, 127–8, 129, 137, 138–40, 142, 144; agrarian undercurrents, 3; guerrilla warfare, 166; massacre of Protestants, 127–8
Wheatley, Hugh, 103
White, General, 41
Whitworth, Lord, 197
Wickham, William, 129, 154, 166
Wicklow (county)
lawless desperados, 158
Military Road, 191–2
rebellion in, 126, 127, 143, 144–5, 150, 166
Wicklow Harbour, 192
William, Prince of Orange, 194
Winter, Henry, 71
Wolfe, Arthur, 1st Viscount Kilwarden, 8, 199

Yelverton, Baron, 104
yeomanry, 50, 97, 100, 135, 154
excesses of, 149

Zimmerman, Captain, 161